EMBRACING

GRACE

A Gospel for All of Us

SCOT MCKNIGHT

PARACLETE PRESS

Brewster, Massachusetts

EMBRACING GRACE: A Gospel for All of Us
2005   *First Printing*

Copyright 2005 by Scot McKnight

ISBN 1-55725-453-2

Library of Congress Cataloging -in- Publication
McKnight, Scot.
Embracing grace : a gospel for all of us / Scot McKnight.
          p.cm.
ISBN 1-55725-453-2
 1. Grace (Theology)   I. Title.
BT761.3.M35 2005
234—dc22   2005016853

10 9 8 7 6 5 4 3 2 1

Published by Paraclete Press
Brewster, Massachusetts
www.paracletepress.com
Printed in the United States of America

FOR

Laura and Mark
Lukas and Annika

CONTENTS

O God, who wonderfully created,
and yet more wonderfully restored,
the dignity of human nature:
Grant that we may share the divine life of him
who humbled himself to share our humanity,
your Son Jesus Christ;
who lives and reigns with you,
in the unity of the Holy Spirit, one God, for ever and ever.
Amen.

Phyllis Tickle
The Divine Hours: Prayers for Autumn and Wintertime

Of Man's First Disobedience, and the Fruit
Of that Forbidden Tree, whose mortal taste
Brought Death into the World, and all our woe,
With loss of Eden, till one Greater Man
Restore us, and regain the blissful Seat.

John Milton
Paradise Lost

There are two occasions when the sacred beauty
of Creation becomes dazzlingly apparent, and they occur together.
One is when we feel our mortal insufficiency to the world,
and the other is when we feel the world's
mortal insufficiency to us.
Theologians talk about prevenient grace that precedes grace
itself and allows us to accept it. I think there must also be a
prevenient courage that allows us to be brave—that is,
to acknowledge that there is more beauty than our eyes can bear,
that previous things have been put into our hands and
to do nothing to honor them is do great harm.

Marilynne Robinson,
Gilead

To put it another way, if there is no point in the story as a whole,
there is no point in my own action.
If the story is meaningless, any action of mine is meaningless.
. . . so the answer to the question "Who am I?" can only be given
if we ask "What is my story?" and that can only be answered
if there is an answer to the further question,
"What is the whole story of which my story is a part?"

Lesslie Newbigin,
The Gospel in a Pluralist Society

PROLOGUE
A Gospel for All of Us

The gospel, above anything else, is the one element of the Christian faith that all Christians can (or should) agree on. After all, it is a gospel *for all of us*—not just for my own segment or your own segment of the Church. It does not belong to one and only one denomination; it belongs to the whole Church. The gospel is the one gift that is for all of us.

Christians today are tired of hearing people announce that one local or denominational church has it all right. We know that none of us has it all right, and we are learning that we need one another. We surely don't agree on everything, but the one thing we can agree on could be the gospel itself.

Many of us today are also tired of "too much talking" and "not enough doing" when it comes to a gospel life. An undeniable feature of the attractiveness of Jesus is that he wasn't distracted by endless debates about theories: he rolled up his sleeves and he invited people to join him in his vision for the kingdom of God. Debates lose much of their heat when you are working side by side with Jesus for the kingdom.

I tell the story of the gospel in what follows, and along the way I tell stories of a variety of persons who discovered that the gospel can soothe suffering and forgive their sins and restore their community and empower them to work for the good of the world. In other words, they learned that the gospel can satisfy the soul. The only two things, G. K. Chesterton once said, "that can satisfy the soul are a person and a story; and even a story must be about a person." The gospel is a story about a Person and about persons who find themselves in that story.

In telling stories of the gospel, however, I will not be giving "proofs" of the gospel. The gospel is good enough on its own, and it doesn't need to be propped up with proofs. Stories are like that. No one needs to prove that *The Adventures of Tom Sawyer* or *The Lord of the Rings* or *Charlotte's Web* are good stories. Read them and you will be drawn in, just as we can be drawn into the gospel story. That is a gift for all of us.

INTRODUCTION
The Gospels Among Us

I f you ask Christian folk, something I occasionally do just
to get a conversation started, "What is the gospel?" you are
more than likely to get one of three answers. If you ask the
question in a spirit of non-defensive curiosity, you are more
than likely to get people to say what they really think. There
are three typical answers to the question "What is the
gospel?"

First, some say this: "The gospel is that Jesus came to earth
to die for my sins so I could be forgiven and go to heaven to
be with God for eternity." Most of the time those who give
this answer to the question also provide a quotation from the
Gospel of John or from Paul's letter to the Roman Christians.

Second, others say this: "The gospel is the Good News that
Jesus came to liberate us from oppression, from systemic evil,
from slavery, so there would be justice and peace." I also hear
this one quite often, and these people tend to quote a line or
two from Jesus' well-known inaugural sermon in Luke chapter
four or from the prophet Micah.

Third, another group says something like this: "The gospel
is being part of the Church." Again, this group will sometimes
quote a Bible verse, but they are just as likely to quote their

pastor or priest and say that they grew up in the Church and that this is what they were taught.

There is no reason here to figure "which group is giving which answer?" or to start pointing fingers at one another. And there is no reason to start claiming that "my gospel is better than your gospel." Instead, there is every reason for us to ask how we got ourselves into this muddle: how, we can be asking, could we have such different approaches to what is so basic? If the gospel is for all of us, how did it come to pass that each group thinks it alone has the gospel figured out? One group emphasizes forgiveness of sins, another the transformation of persons and society, and the other our inclusion in the community of faith. Is there a right and a wrong with these answers?

The most important thing I have to say in Embracing Grace *is this:* each of these groups is trying to say the same thing, each of these groups is right in what they do say about the gospel, and each of these groups needs the definition of the other. But first we need to define the gospel groups.

SO WHAT IS THE GOSPEL?

Embracing Grace is written because of my experiences teaching in churches across the United States and in classrooms with students who come to my school (North Park University) from a variety of backgrounds. Each semester in my classes I have students who are Protestant, who are Roman Catholic, and who are Eastern Orthodox. I have students who are charismatic, who are liturgical, and those who don't know what either of those terms means. I've done my best to listen to them and to get these students to engage Christians from other traditions, and I've always asked them to look again at the Bible to see what it says about the gospel. *Embracing Grace* flows from this interaction.

It is my conviction that God designed the gospel to be a source of communion for all Christians and not a source of division among them. But this communion can emerge only if we respect one another enough to listen to what the other is saying, and if we go back to the Bible *together* to see what the gospel really is. So, how would I define the gospel?

The gospel is the work of God to restore humans to union with God and communion with others, in the context of a community, for the good of others and the world. This is what I call the gospel of "embracing grace." In this book we will look at each element of this definition, tweaking it here and there with special words. This is a general summary of a gospel *for all of us.* It tells the story of a God who embraces us in spite of who we are and what we have done; it tells us that God's embrace enables us to embrace God back and to embrace others, and that this double embrace is intended for the good of others and the world. This grace comes to us in Jesus

Christ, in his death and resurrection, and in the gift of the Holy Spirit.

So, when I use "embracing grace" in this book, I am referring to the unleashing of an endless cycle of grace that can end what Philip Yancey calls the "cycle of ungrace" in our hearts and world. Here is the flow of grace:

God embraces you and me and
God embraces others and
God embraces the whole created order.

Then:

You and I embrace God back and
We embrace others and
We embrace the entire created order.

The gospel is designed to create this cycle of grace. Each of the "gospels" among us that we have just mentioned focuses on one element of the definition above or on one element or more of the cycle of grace, but each of those gospels could benefit from listening to the others. Indeed, the gospel is about forgiveness, about justice, and about the community of faith. And it is about each of them, together.

Embracing Grace invites each of us to listen to one another and prays that in listening we will learn from one another and grow into a deeper unity.

Embracing Grace

EMBRACING GRACE

1
PERFORMING
THE GOSPEL

THE GOSPEL IS MORE LIKE A PIECE OF MUSIC to be performed than a list of ideas to endorse. Embracing grace invites us to listen to each line of the gospel creed, digest each line, and then transform the lines into a life lived in the here and now. Thus, it is a gospel that is both proclaimed *and* performed. The first without the latter is hypocrisy; the second without the first is not the gospel. But, together they tell God's story so satisfyingly that others are compelled to join along.

Jesus entered into Galilee and gave himself as a person to love and as a life to be followed. The doctrines, which clearly were involved, flowed out of the love and the following. To claim that the gospel is more than a creed does not diminish creeds but puts them in their proper place. Whether we look at Jesus' message of the kingdom or the apostle Paul's glorious theology of grace, each is designed to transform life as it is lived in the here and now. Jesus measured people by how they lived because he was concerned with character. In fact, how a person lived showed what they really believed. "[B]y their fruit," Jesus said in the Sermon on the Mount, "you will know them."

Sometimes I ask students to read the prophets after they have read Paul's letter to the Romans. Paul articulates theology and the prophets inform us that theology isn't what it is supposed to be until it is lived. Of course, Paul says this, too, but sometimes it takes time with a prophet to know what the apostle is saying.

A STORY WE PERFORM

A lot of people in this world are looking for a place where the gospel of embracing grace transcends proclamation and becomes performance, and when they see it performed, they join in. Why? Because when the gospel is embodied it tells the gospel story better than anything Hollywood can flash on the screen and better than any novelist can put on paper. The reason the gospel has been around as long as it has been, besides Providence itself, is that it tells our story better than we can tell our own.

But people today don't want either a glitzy or a tame gospel. Ordinary, perhaps; but tame, no. We don't mind being told that the gospel story can be like Marilynne Robinson's *Gilead,* a story in which an ordinary pastor passes an ordinary life with ordinary people and wants to tell his son about his ordinary story. Nor do we mind being told that the gospel can be as difficult as Ernest Hemingway's character Santiago in *The Old Man and the Sea,* who finally catches the big fish, but by the time he gets home he only has the story to tell rather than the big fish to sell—or eat or show off!

Furthermore, we don't want to be told that the gospel will all of a sudden solve all our problems and make the world shine its happy face on us from sunup to sundown. We don't want anyone to tell us a gospel like this because we know it isn't true. And we don't want to be told that the gospel is about being nice to one another, or that if we sit down for a little conference on peace, the world will be a better place. New winds are blowing, and these winds are asking the Church for a gospel that not only forgives my sin but also works for justice and peace and does so in a meaningful community where we both hear about and experience the love Jesus called his followers to have.

This generation wants an authentic gospel, one that is both proclamation and performance, a gospel that deals with the world they live in: a world that is full of images of people dying and starving and being put to death by goons, a world where there is a profusion of tensions, a world where the Christian faith isn't the only faith in town, a world where one particular denomination doesn't own the market on everything, a world where neighborhoods don't look like the one in *The Waltons.* An authentic gospel creates, as Pastor John Burke says so well in his *No Perfect People Allowed,* a culture where you come as you are and drop phoniness and pretense as you pass through the doors. Such a culture, he contends, is one of trust, of tolerance, of truth, one that takes persons in who are broken and alone. No wonder attendance at Burke's Gateway Church has skyrocketed.

A come-as-you-are culture, within the walls of the Church, as Burke describes it, will develop permeable walls. Such walls don't separate between believers and unbelievers, but invite everyone to come to the table to listen to Jesus. Such walls don't separate between denominations, between young and old, between the poor and the wealthy, between the morally struggling and good old-fashioned upright people, between men and women, between ethnic groups and cultural climates.

Instead, permeable walls permit entrance and exit without notice and without judgment. A come-as-you-are culture in not indiscriminate, but it creates a church where grace is the ruling paradigm. It asks people to tell their story and promises them safety and love. When permeable walls are found, honesty is found—sometimes frank, but honesty nonetheless. Permeable walls may be walls, but you don't know they are there.

This generation—the sort of people you and I pass on the road in our commutes or bump into in the aisles at the grocery store or who may go to bed cold and lonely, or who wake up one morning to cancer or to someone's tragic death or who live their three score and ten—this generation doesn't want something that tells them that everything is good. It wants something more and won't settle for anything less. I sense an impatience with the Church's neat divisions into denominations and an urgency to start something new. This generation doesn't want to attend church in nice clothes, drop some small-numbered bills into the collection plate, sing "When the roll is called up yonder I'll be there," and go home—that is, after a nice meal at a nice restaurant. And it really doesn't care what the church calls itself or what denomination it belongs to.

A stronger way of saying it is this: this generation is challenging the Church to perform what it proclaims, or, to use less elegant language, to put up or shut up.

What this generation is asking to see proclaimed by performance is grace.

People today want to get to the bottom of things, in fact to the bottom of their own things. They want something that finds what is really there and tells them there is a way for what is really there to be restored to what it once was or what it can be. They want something that speaks to their condition and that can set them free from the chaos this world confronts them with. They want something that will draw them closer to God and to others and lead them to a life that is good for the world. And they want to both hear it and see it.

This come-as-you-are generation wants to see if the Church really does love them.

PATRICK OF IRELAND

One of the most compelling pictures of a live-it-out gospel is the story of Saint Patrick of Ireland. When a teenager, the son of a wealthy and powerful Christian pillar of a community in Britain, Patrick was kidnapped. His dream of a life of fame and wealth was jolted in the middle of the night by voices and weapons and threats. He was gagged and wrapped in chains. Then he and others in the household were marched in the dead of night to a waiting boat. Each of those captured was summarily evaluated in a cold-blooded triage, and some, because they were deemed useless to the mission, were put to

Embracing Grace

death in the sight of the young man, searing his mind with images too vivid to allow sleep. Patrick himself survived the triage only because he was robust enough for farming.

Forced into a boat and taken into exile in a foreign country, Patrick became the slave of a sheep farmer for six years. Reared in a wealthy home and promised a noble future, he found himself laboring on a primitive farm in a foreign country. Instead of a future, Patrick had a past. But, in that exile this is what he wrote: "But it was here . . . that God first opened my heart. . . . God used the time to shape and mold me into something better. He made me into what I am now—someone very different from what I once was, someone who can care about others and work to help them. Before I was a slave, I didn't even care about myself." Patrick found his story in God's embracing grace.

As a slave with plenty of time to reflect on the meaning of life, Patrick reclaimed the Christian faith he had recently renounced for atheism. He began to rise early to say his prayers fastidiously, and he began a lifelong practice of fasting. He used his time tending sheep for prayer and for reciting the Bible stories he had learned as a child. Before long, Patrick the slave was being called "holy boy." So intense were his prayers that he received a vision: in his dream God told him that he would be going home soon and that a boat was ready. That boat, however, was some two hundred miles away.

Somehow Patrick escaped, shrewdly found passage across the sea, and wended his way back to his home and his family. There he had yet another dream in which God spoke to him. Only this time the dream involved a call to return to the land of his slavery to preach the gospel and establish churches. His family thought he was crazy, but Patrick went anyway (after a brief theological education).

In that land of Hibernia, Patrick, a freshly anointed preacher, and his growing number of fellow Christians established church after church through both proclamation of the simple truth and performance of the simple life in a community. Leader after leader embraced the gospel, and community after community experienced its restoring powers. The marginalized, especially women, found meaning and were empowered by the story of God's embracing grace. Patrick ministered to the whole person—heart, soul, mind, and body. This revival under Patrick occurred in the fifth century AD. His parish was northern Ireland. Today we call him St. Patrick of Ireland, and the whole church claims Patrick because his was an authentic, credible gospel.

CHURCHES PERFORM THE GOSPEL

We don't get to choose between performing or not performing the gospel.

A local church *always* performs the gospel it proclaims. This may sound odd, so let me emphasize the word "always." A church *always* performs the gospel it proclaims because its performance is its proclamation. If you look at a church and what it does and how it operates you will *see* the gospel of that church. The important point to make here is that the deepest indicator of that church's gospel cannot be limited to the pastor's sermons, or the Sunday school teachers' teaching, or the doctrinal statement's affirmations, or the summer camp offerings, or the aesthetic expressions. The sure indicator of the gospel in a local community is how those Christians live.

If the local church is loving or unloving, or if it responds to the community's needs or doesn't even know about them, or if it is as racially mixed as the community or if it has only one racial make-up in an multi-ethnic community, or if it has great music and splendidly dressed pastors, or if it has lots of rules to follow and lines to sign, then that is what the church is actually preaching.

The performed gospel is the gospel the local community proclaims. *Always.* Which is why a church like NorthBridge, on the border of Illinois and Wisconsin, is making an impact in its community.

NORTHBRIDGE

Tucked into a public building at the corner of highways 173 and 83 in Antioch, Illinois, is NorthBridge Church. The pastor is Mark Albrecht and the worship leader is his wife, Michelle. NorthBridge is a new faith community, and so it has faced all the usual issues, including that of building a facility. But, instead of spending their funds right away to construct a building, the people chose a different option. The money given in many local churches is nearly exhausted by building expenses, salaries, and fees, with very little (if any) left for the community. But NorthBridge's people did something else: they tilted their ears to see if there were needs they could attend to. That is where they began.

When Mark, along with other church leaders in the area, heard about the financial crisis in the Grass Lake school district, Mark approached the Superintendent, Jim Beveridge, and asked what they could do. Jim informed Mark that an old school building did not meet the building code and was no longer usable, and that it would cost over a quarter of a million dollars to rehabilitate it. The district needed that building. Mark and the leaders convened, prayed, and came up with a plan: they decided to fix the building, not by hiring it out, but with volunteer labor from their own church and other communities of faith in the area. Together—a word local

Embracing Grace

churches often struggle with—they fixed that old building, and the costs were about a tenth of the original estimate because of volunteer labor.

Church work and community work, forgiveness of sins and justice, and gospel ministry and social ministry got all wound up into one effort. Instead of concentrating on "church work," instead of pouring scorn on the local school administrators, instead of family frustration leading to a move to another town, instead of raising funds for another private Christian school, these churches entered the public square and did what they could to help—and they got "nothing" out of it. Giving is like that.

They also got nothing out of ShareFest, another community event they orchestrated. Several in NorthBridge discovered a bundle of needs, most of them unmet and low on someone's priority list. They organized ShareFest. Junior and Senior high school students painted 557 fire hydrants, others painted a public works building, some winterized and restored senior citizens' homes. Others worked in the local wetlands. They held a clothing and food drive and a blood drive, as well as a musical performance. Albrecht was quoted in the local *Antioch Press:* "We went out and asked, 'How can we help?' It was kind of revolutionary." ShareFest ended with a community-wide celebration service, in which all the pastors and congregations participated. Proclamation led to performance, and the proclamation was made credible *because* it was performed.

Mark Albrecht and NorthBridge are not doing this alone; they do not want attention. Pastor Albrecht simply wants to see the story of embracing grace performed at NorthBridge Church for the good of Antioch and the glory of God. It is exciting work, and many other churches, both old and new, are catching a new vision of the old gospel story, the gospel preached by Patrick and the gospel performed in Antioch.

SOLOMON'S PORCH

This is why I find an avant-garde church in Minneapolis, Solomon's Porch, so suggestive of what the local church can be. I am not suggesting that other churches are not just as suggestive, for I have given and will give other churches as examples. The pastor—and "pastor" is too strong a term for his liking—of Solomon's Porch, Doug Pagitt, decided to write up what goes on in this innovative faith community over the period of a week, and the narrative of *Reimagining Spiritual Formation* unfolds a multitude of ideas and provocative suggestions for what the church could be in a local community.

What I like most about Solomon's Porch is that it has as its goal the formation of a community that embodies the gospel. Here's how Pagitt says it: "To be honest, the legitimacy of what we're doing at Solomon's Porch will be best judged in 15 to 20 years. . . . The question that haunts me is not, 'Do people like our church?' but 'Is there any real formation happening?' Two decades from now, will our efforts at human formation be shown to have contributed to the lives we have led for the past 20 years? . . . When we move beyond belief-based faith to life-lived, holistic faith, the only true test is lives lived over time."

Proclamation and performance of an authentic gospel combine into credibility.

2

THE BEGINNING OF
THE GOSPEL

THE GOSPEL BEGINS AT THE BIBLE'S BEGINNING. If we fail to begin there, we will miss the gospel.

Genesis 1:1 tells us that God created the heavens and the earth, and in the next verse that the cosmos was *tohu va-bohu,* "a formless void." Then God's (Michelangelo-like) finger reaches out, touches the swirling and whirling chaos of *tohu va-bohu,* and turns it all into order. Chaotic commotion becomes ordered motion. Part of turning the *tohu va-bohu* into order, in fact the apex of God's order-making, is creating man and woman, Adam and Eve. They appear on the last day of God's creative work. For them God prepared a little world called Eden and asked them to take care of it.

Plenty of Christians worry about whether or not the early chapters of Genesis are straightforward history or not, and some even speculate on the DNA of Adam and Eve. What is more important about Adam and Eve for *Embracing Grace* is not their DNA but that they were made in the image of God, what I will call the *Eikon* of God. This is where the gospel begins.

EIKONS OF GOD

Only after God made Adam and Eve did God say, "This is very good." The stupendous element about Adam and Eve is that they were made, according to Genesis chapter one, "in our [God's] *image, according to our likeness.*" Genesis was originally written in Hebrew and then much later translated into Greek. The Hebrew word translated as "image" is *tselem,* and the Greek translation is *Eikon.* I will use *Eikon* throughout *Embracing Grace* since "image of God," the more customary Christian expression, has been over-used and become diluted by academic debates. (And the word *tselem* hasn't caught on.)

Most of us connect to the term *Eikon.* Many of us will think of "icons" on computer screens. When we click on them we enter another screen. Others will think of the "icons" in Orthodox churches or in the museums of this world. They, too, are designed by their creators to lead us into something else—in this case to God. I will use *Eikon* because, since it is rarely used, it gives us a new term to think with. By using a new term we will be able to fill it with its own meaning.

When God made humans, he gave them hearts, souls, minds, bodies, and wills to make them *individuals;* God gave them other individuals just like themselves so they could live in *community;* and he gave them a *world* in which to live. Into this world God set Adam and Eve to be Eikons, to be visible bodies that reflect the glory of God. As the *Westminster Larger Catechism* put it so well in the opening question:

1. What is the chief and highest end [goal] of man [humans]?
   A: Man's chief and highest end is *to glorify God,* and fully to enjoy him forever.

John Piper, pastor and theologian, suggested that *"and* fully to enjoy him forever" be changed to *"by* enjoying him forever." God's joy is ours and ours is God's.

As Eikons of God, God has given us the opportunity to explore the world. For us to do this God gave us two gifts: *freedom* and *relationships with others.* Freedom, the freedom to do or not to do what God said, is inherent to being human. In addition to giving us freedom, God made more than one person, creating both male and female, so people would learn to love one another. So relationship is also inherent to what

Embracing Grace

it means to be an Eikon of God. The Genesis account tells that after God made Adam he said, "It is not good that the man should be alone." Humans, both Adams and Eves, are designed for relationships. Those relationships are Godward (loving God) and otherward (loving others), and both are to occur within the world in which we live (loving creation).

Here then we have the context of being an Eikon of God: we are individuals who are inherently like God and like one another so we can love God and love others, and we are to do all this in the place where God puts us—right here on earth, and for its good. The eighth Psalm says this beautifully: "what are human beings that you are mindful of them? . . . Yet you have made them a little lower than God, and crowned them with glory and honor. You have given them dominion over the works of your hands."

The gospel is about every one of these dimensions of human life—the human's relationship to herself and himself, to God, to others, and to the world and to the society in which we live. That gospel begins when we realize, as Mister Rogers did, that humans are special.

MEET MISTER FRED ROGERS

When my children were young they loved to watch *Mister Rogers' Neighborhood,* so Kris and I frequently watched Mister Rogers with them. His slow pace was accompanied by chatter about feelings and that it is all right to have such feelings. I thought he had some quirky manners, and I didn't care much for his funky shoes and old-fashioned cardigan. We knew at the time that Fred Rogers was an ordained Presbyterian minister, but I confess I was at times put off by his constant mantra about being "you" or being "special." But I was wrong. Fred Rogers was seeking to instill into children something integral to the entire sweep of Christian theology: that humans are Eikons of God, special, and capable of *being* a message. As Bob Faw on the NBC *Nightly News* reported after Fred Rogers died, "The real Mister Rogers never preached, [never] even mentioned God [on his show]. He never had to."

No one has told the story of Fred Rogers better than Amy Hollingsworth. An only child, "Fat Freddy" Rogers was weak and got picked on. So he played alone. He learned to express his negative feelings about life through piano playing and puppet characters. His personal experiences along with his study of psychology and theology filled him with a unique capacity to understand the inner world of children, and he sensed that children needed help—which they did and still do and always will.

In seminary, Fred Rogers learned that there are two kinds of Christian leaders: "accusers" and "advocates." He chose to be the latter, and this explains why his life was a story of embracing grace. What buoyed up his choice of being an advocate was that he had learned the Eikonic nature of humans, what he called the "divine sacredness and otherness and holiness that we find in God in our neighbor." He sustained this advocacy role of helping children grow into healthy human beings by rising at 5 AM for prayer, reflection, and Bible reading, and then a 7:30 AM swim at the pool (who will forget the day on TV when he "showed off" that pathetic body in a Speedo?), and he retired by 9:30 PM. He mentioned his friends by name when he was their advocate in prayer.

When Fred Rogers received an honorary doctorate at Boston University in 1992, he was asked to come up to give the invocation, but before he could get there the students broke into wild and uncontrolled chanting of his name. Flustered, he simply asked if they'd like to sing, and sing they did: "It's a beautiful day in the neighborhood. . . ." Mister Rogers, so I believe, gave to a generation or two of kids a profound sense of their specialness, of their Eikonic status, and showed that we are made to live out this life in our neighborhood.

If the gospel is for all of us, Mister Rogers would have given a special emphasis to the word "for."

INDIVIDUALS OR EIKONS?

The entire Judaeo-Christian tradition, whether we think in terms of politics, economics, or law, believes humans are special—that they are Eikons. But since the Enlightenment there has been a steady erosion at the foundations of how humans perceive one another and how we perceive ourselves: humans, who were once seen as the glory of God's creation, are being diminished by ideologies, laws, and political power plays.

Peter Speckhard, Senior Pastor of Faith Lutheran Church in Green Bay, Wisconsin, at a national convention, concluded his sermon "Who Made Thee?" with the following challenge to the Church, a challenge that summons us to begin our gospel by embracing our "made in God's image" status:

> Some say I am DNA. Some say I am a product of my society. Some say I am merely a smart animal, a mass of brainwaves, or a calculating will to power. The evolutionary biologist, the psychologist, the environmentalist, the biochemist, the sociologist, the economist, the Ivy-League ethicist, they all call me something. But you in the Church, who do you say that I am?

The Christian should stand up and shout out, "Peter, you are an Eikon"! C. S. Lewis's oft-quoted words may express this better than anything I've ever seen or heard: "Next to the Blessed Sacrament itself, your neighbor is the holiest object presented to your senses." The gospel begins right here.

But, in the vast majority of post-Enlightenment perceptions of human nature, whether they are political or scientific or interpersonal or institutional or familial, human beings are understood first and foremost as *individuals.* While I would not want to say that being an individual is unchristian or somehow wrong, the focal point of the Bible—from Genesis to Revelation—is elsewhere. The focal point of the entire tradition is that humans need to be seen as Eikons. Seeing humans as merely *individuals* diminishes the well-rounded Eikon of God. It is to exclude our relationship to God and our relationships to others from the discussion, and that leaves each of us stranded as we determine who we are.

Individualism is the biggest obstacle to the gospel of embracing grace.

WHAT IS INDIVIDUALISM?

Individualism tells us we are on our own, and we might be able to make it on our own. Individualism makes God and others into commodities we choose to further our own ends. Individualism diminishes who we are made to be.

In Andrew Delbanco's sketch of American social history, *The Real American Dream,* we move through three periods in our nation's development: God, Nation, and Self. He says of our current era in history, the Era of the Self, that because our culture is so self-absorbed "the modern self becomes all and nothing at the same time." The irony is that individualism diminishes each of us. Amitai Etzioni, in a study on the pursuit of individualism that runs from Jean-Jacques Rousseau, Ralph Waldo Emerson, and Walt Whitman right into the Era of Self, concludes with this: "Individualism promises those who believe in it that they are free-standing agents, able to formulate their own conceptions of the good, pursue a life that is guided by reasonable deliberations, and render rational decisions in their self-interest. And, as bearers of inalienable rights, they have a long list of entitlements, but no inherent duties or obligations unless they choose to embrace them."

Notice these words: "no inherent duties or obligations." Individualism diminishes us because it backs away from commitment and community. If humans are made to relate to God and to others, individualism attacks our very essence. Commitment to civic institutions, commentators like Delbanco are saying, is waning: we find people "bowling alone" and watching TV too much and sitting at home with few contacts with neighbors. People don't vote as they ought, and no one cares any more about civic holidays. Many social historians today blame this on the individualism that has been passed on to us.

Some people flip-flop to the other side and believe we are mere cogs in a collective wheel, where the wheel determines everything. Others flop-flip into another simplistic place and think everything is deterministic—God is in control, as if God were dangling puppets in some tragedy or comedy.

But the real problem in the Western world is individualism. Instead, we need to see ourselves as individuals, but part of a larger community through which God is working. Different eras tilt in one direction or another, and ours is one that has tilted lopsidedly toward individualism.

EIKONS ARE MADE TO EMBRACE

The gospel, however, strikes a perfect balance—one in which God, others, and the individual *relate to one another in love,* but they do so in such a way that their individual integrity is protected. The Bible begins with humans in union with God and communion with others and the world, and so offers to us a counter-cultural alternative—a concept that is so attractive to many of our generation. Instead of being individuals, the Bible says, we are Eikons. Instead of part of a collective, we are in a *community.* Instead of God being a determinist, God shares his love and gives us the *freedom* to enjoy that love.

We are by nature Eikons—humans designed to relate to God and others for the good of our world. This is what we are by nature.

Lukas and Annika, our son and his wife, have a Cairn Terrier named Slater. We have a Bichon Frise named Webster. The dogs' natures are wildly different. If I am in a new place with Webster and I open a door, he walks gingerly to the opening and inquires rather suspiciously about what might be in there. It takes some coasting and coaching to get him to enter the room. "Ask questions before you act" is his approach. When I am with Slater, who has more chutzpah than his little body needs, in a new place, and a door opens, he charges through it to experience what is in there. "Act and ask questions later" is his approach. By nature, Cairn Terriers are curious and exploratory and fearless. Open a door for them and they see an opportunity. By nature, Bichon Frises are friendly and sedate and cautious. Open a door for them and they see a risk. By nature, Slater is alert; by nature, Webster is asleep. By nature, Slater barks; by nature, Webster wonders.

Humans are by nature Eikons: that is who we are. By nature, we are designed with the inalienable right to be embraced and to embrace: embracing God who made us and embracing ourselves, embracing others, and embracing our world.

The gospel that tells our story begins with this beginning.

3

THE STORY OF THE EIKON

MISTER ROGERS BELIEVED HUMANS WERE SPECIAL, and everything he did made that belief visible. Leo Tolstoy believed in the kingdom of God, but his life rarely showed his belief. Why, we want to ask, did Tolstoy struggle so much in performing so badly what he boldly proclaimed and for which he was willing to suffer?

Tolstoy, whose power to tell stories knows no rival, fell from his elevated status among the literary elite when he was converted to a utopian vision of the kingdom of God on earth. In this utopia, Tolstoy idealized the life of a simple peasant working in a society of peace. Knowing no other way to make his points clear, Tolstoy argued for his vision in regular diatribes against the demands of the flesh and private property. But it only takes a few minutes with the letters and diaries of Leo Tolstoy to realize that the kingdom he believed in and argued for rarely found its way into his personal life.

Those who follow the life of Tolstoy know that he died in 1910 in a cottage across the tracks from the forlorn train station in Astapovo. He was eighty-two years old. He died in Astapovo because he was fleeing from life with his wife at their large estate at Yasnaya Polyana. Leo and his wife, Sonya, were daily foes and daily companions. As William Shirer, a chronicler of these episodes, puts it: "Day after day, year after year, they put down their innermost and increasingly bitter thoughts about the other. And for years they left what they wrote for the other to read—it was a perverse form of communication between them."

Here is a typical entry from their diaries. *Sonya:* "It turned into another painful conversation, with yet more recriminations. I was in tears almost all day. Leo Nikolayevich [Tolstoy] is in a terrible state: he torments both himself and me." Answering back, *Leo:* "Slept badly, very little. Spoke to Sonya about the [forester staying on the estate] and there was the usual emotion and irritation. I am very depressed. I keep wanting to cry." For years, day after day, this was the true story of Tolstoy's life. Yet, as that story was

Embracing Grace

performed, Tolstoy was dreaming and writing about peace and the kingdom of God.

It would be easy to write Tolstoy off as another example of a hypocrite, someone whose life didn't perform the story of his faith. But, to dismiss Tolstoy as a hypocrite deprives us of the opportunity to dig deeper. Below the level of hypocrisy lies this question: why does a brilliant novelist who longs for and can describe a peaceful utopia, a nonviolent one at that, find himself so full of vile emotion and violent anger and venomous rhetoric? Because the story of humans is about beings who can be *both* brilliant *and* bad. That is "the story we find ourselves in," to use the title of Brian McLaren's theological novel. The story of the good and bad is the gospel story.

Tolstoy's story is that of the turbulent heart that points its compass at hope and peace and love and the kingdom of God, but struggles to make it happen. And we can get to that kingdom only by entering into the turbulent heart of authentic humans. In his long-sentence prose Brian Doyle reflects on the heart of all humans. Humans, he says, carry with them a heart filled with all kinds of pain.

I think about this all the time. I find myself staring at the shoulders of counselors and priests and doctors and mothers, to see what the weight looks like. I find myself thinking that most people sure are extraordinary. I find myself thinking, as I get older and less cocky and less sure and more merciful and more hip to the fact that everyone has scars on their hearts and will, and everyone carries loads or will, and everyone carries their load alone or will, that maybe all people are extraordinary, whether or not I see that clear, and that my seeing it or not seeing it has nothing to do with the reality of grace under duress, which is pretty much the story of the human race. Love carries a lot of pain in its chest.

This is the story we find ourselves in. In the loving chest of humans is pain; in every chest there is brilliance and badness. We find in humans around us a glory that astounds as well as a frailty that can shatter. What story can put this story into words? There is no more resonant answer to that question, I believe, than the biblical story of the Eikon.

THE STORY OF THE EIKON

There are four chapters in the story of the *Eikon*. In the first chapter, which we can read at the beginning of the Bible, humans are created as Eikons of God. In the second chapter, the Eikon cracks (Genesis 3). After the creation and the cracking, the next chapter tells the story of Jesus, the perfect Eikon. The final chapter is eternity: here we see the Eikon united in love with God and others in a perfect Eden. Nothing captures this quite like the last two chapters of the Bible. Differences aside, both Protestants and Roman Catholics call this final chapter of the story of the Eikon "glorification," while the Orthodox call it "union with God" or *theosis.*

The third chapter of this story is the most important one for understanding the gospel: Jesus is himself described by the apostle Paul as the *Eikon of God.* Paul, in the fourth chapter of his second letter to the Corinthians, speaks to us about the "gospel of the glory of Christ, who is the Eikon of God." Just a few lines earlier he says that Christians are those who "are being transformed into the same Eikon, from one degree of glory to another." And in the first chapter of the letter to the Hebrews, the author says that Jesus is "the reflection of God's glory and the exact imprint of God's very being." The implication of Jesus' being the perfect human is enormous: God's work for us is to make us like Christ. Jesus is the perfect Eikon and the gospel is designed to transform humans into that Eikon.

This is theoretical, and we are entitled to ask if it makes a difference now. My answer is, "Absolutely."

WHAT DOES IT MEAN TO BE AN EIKON NOW?

For nearly two thousand years, theologians have been discussing what the Eikon means. Nearly every one of these discussions compares humans to the animal kingdom in order to discover *what makes humans superior to animals.*

One such distinction is found in the first chapter of Genesis, when God says we are to "have dominion" over the rest of the created order. These words could suggest that being an Eikon refers to our calling to govern creation. But, if you were to ask elephants or peregrine falcons or Hudson Bay polar bears or ivory-billed woodpeckers or pandas or ocelots or the Alabama red-bellied turtle, each would raise a foot or paw or claw or wing to vote for new governors. If this is what it means to be an Eikon then we have some confessions to make. Others, still comparing humans to the animal kingdom, have suggested that Eikon refers to the natural superior intelligence of humans, or to the ability of humans to relate to one another in love, or to the human capacity for spirituality, or to humans' having self-consciousness and a moral sense.

It is unwise to reject all this good thinking. But, in addition to asking what makes humans different from the rest of creation we should also ask another question, which I think is both more important and more revealing: what makes us *like God?* The Bible tells us that we are made as Eikons of *God,* not Eikons of *creation.*

If we ask how we are like God, we begin to answer that question by asking, "What does God *do?*" And what God does in the opening chapters of the Bible is pretty clear: God *creates* and God *relates* and God *rests.* If this is what God does, and we are like God, then to be an Eikon means we "create" order out of chaos—which is what my wife, Kris, does every time she enters the kitchen after I have cooked and made a *tohu va-bohu* out of the stove and sink and floor and table. It means that we are Eikons when we relate to one another and the world, and (yes, this too) when we rest. To be like God means we are co-creators, co-relators, and co-resters. As Eikons we are "like" God and we are at the same time "different from" the rest of the created order.

There is one more consideration, and it is the most exciting element of all: not only do we ask how we are different from creation and like God in what God *does,* but we ask this: "Who *is* God?" It is here that we brush up against the mystery of God, the Eikon, and the gospel.

PERICHORESIS:
THE HEART OF GOD

Who God *is* has been studied by many theologians, including America's most famous theologian, Jonathan Edwards. When George Marsden, his biographer, summarized a series of sermons Edwards preached on love in the eighteenth century, he discovered that at the heart of Edwards's theology was the view that "the very essence of [God's] reality . . . was the intratrinitarian love of the Father, Son, and Holy Spirit. The only possible reason for such a perfect being to create the universe was to extend that love to other, imperfect, beings." "All created reality," Edwards continued, "is like a quintessential explosion of light from the sun of God's inter-trinitarian love." Creation itself, in the view of Jonathan Edwards, is God's desire to extend God's own being of pulsating love into other created matter. The implication of this line of thinking is this: if creation is God's extending *who God is,* then our Eikonic status suddenly becomes an expression of who God is!

This theological idea is called the *perichoresis,* and we will turn to this term from time to time to help our explanation of the gospel. *Perichoresis* goes back to the Gospel of John and was later explained more completely by one of the first theologians of Asia Minor, Gregory of Nyssa. John tells us in chapter ten that Jesus said, "the Father is in me and I am in the Father." The doctrine of the perichoresis teaches that God exists as an interpenetrating and mutual indwelling of the persons of the Trinity. In other words, God's eternal reality is the love between Father, Son, and Holy Spirit. This is what God was doing, is doing now, and will do for eternity. This is what God *is.* Eikons are an expression of that reality and designed for that reality only. The gospel is designed to lead humans into that interpenetrating and mutually indwelling love of God.

Here's the sum of it all: if God's nature is this interpenetrating perichoresis of personal love, then the Eikon of God is most what it is supposed to be when it too is embraced by

God and embraces others and the world. We are most human when we are dwelling in the perichoretic love of God, when we are dancing to the music of God's love. Union and communion are the goal of all created reality. Anyone touched by Jesus is transformed into this loving communion, and the transformation will spread to all of our relationships. So much so that the apostle Paul can say to the Galatians, in the third chapter, that "[t]here is no longer Jew or Greek, there is no longer slave or free, there is no longer male and female." In our world we may fail to grasp the leap the apostle Paul is making here; it is found in two words: "no longer." No longer is there division; communion is the goal of the gospel.

Now it is clear why *individualism* is so important in our understanding of the gospel: individualism wrecks the gospel story. Individualism preaches non-communion and the limited value of relationships. Eikons are made as male and female in need of communion with others. It was not good for Adam to be alone; aloneness is not what Eikons are made for. They are designed for relationship. The gospel says this is what life is all about.

I love Dante's famous *Divine Comedy*. If with me you travel beyond *Inferno* and through *Purgatorio* into *Paradiso*, you will come upon his breathtaking understanding of God as the triune Being of Light. Here is the doctrine of the perichoresis in verse form:

In the deep and bright essence of that exalted Light,
   three circles
appeared to me; they had three different colors,
but all of them were of the same dimension;
one circle seemed reflected by the second,
as rainbow is by rainbow, and the third
seemed fire breathed equally by those two circles.

Eternal Light, You only dwell within
Yourself, and only You know You; Self-knowing,
Self-known, You love and smile upon Yourself!

Yes, Mister Rogers, you got it right: we are special. The reason we are special is that we came from this three-circled splendor of loving Light that also draws us back into that Light so that we might be restored by embracing grace.

The story of the Eikon derives absolutely and only from the very beginning, God's own inner perichoretic dance of love, Dante's three Circles of Light dancing amongst themselves in such a manner that one is not sure which is which. We can now slightly modify our opening definition of the gospel: the gospel is the work of the *triune, interpersonal God* to restore Eikons to God and others into that divine communion, and to unleash it into the rest of the world.

Embracing Grace

4
CRACKED
EIKONS

ONCE, WHEN THE SNOW WAS DEEP, and I was with my friend
Mike, we hatched a plot. Mike lived along a busy street,
where there was a big intersection and a large patch of bushes
in his front yard near the street, and we were out of things to
do. We decided to make a small mound of snowballs, stack
them in the bushes in a small pyramid, and when the cars came
along, throw the snowballs at cars from inside the bushes.

But, our plan was more sinister than that. We knew the
traffic pattern. Cars would pile up behind one another at the
stoplight, and then when the light turned green, they'd all

take off. We decided that we would wait until the light turned green, throw snowballs at the unsuspecting cars. We assumed they couldn't stop because the cars behind them would start honking. Even more sinister: as soon as we emptied the pyramid of snowballs, we could run alongside his house, vanish around the back, and climb stairs into a small building, where we would not be discovered.

Again, more sinister. We decided we would target old biddies, because they would be the least likely to turn around and come back after us.

Our plan worked perfectly. We shaped and stored our snowballs, waited until there were plenty of cars, watched for the green light—there it was, and we rose with snowballs and just flat-out peppered the cars. Boom! boom! boom! Sound of brakes. Honk! Honk! Angry driver. Startled, too. Another driver looked at us, pointed the finger that mattered, but drove on. We took off for safety in utter jubilation, such as only twelve-year-old boys know. After doing this three or four times we were exhausted, but so full of ourselves we decided to do it one more time before "retiring" for the evening. The plan worked again.

What we didn't plan on was that someone would call the police, who would send "The Fuzz" to the corner where it was reported that boys were slamming snowballs into the sides of unsuspecting cars. Unbeknownst to either Mike or me, this was happening as we parted ways and I began my walk home. On my way, an officer pulled up beside me and asked me where I had been. I said, "at a friend's." What had I been doing? "Watching cartoons," I lied. Had I been throwing snowballs or had I seen any boys throwing snowballs at cars? No, I hadn't been throwing snowballs, neither had I seen anyone throwing snowballs at cars. What was in my hand? (No kidding) It was a snowball. He asked to see my gloves, which were sopping wet from playing in the snow. He suggested that I had probably not been watching TV, which I confessed was probably true. Trained in criminal logic, he suggested that I had probably been playing in the snow and throwing snowballs. The "at cars" came along swiftly after his previous suggestion. "Busted!" would be the word. He then told me to get in the car, and asked where I lived, and he took me home (nice officer, don't you think?) and had a little chat with my father, and before long I was in trouble with my father and my mother as well as "The Fuzz."

Like Augustine's exploring his own sinfulness through the experience of stealing pears as a child, I can confess that our action had all the earmarks of a son of Adam and the story of a diminished Eikon. I knew it was wrong and I did it anyway. Both of us knew it was wrong, and we egged one another on. We knew we could damage cars, and we didn't care. We knew our parents had told us not to do this, and we did it anyway. Our teachers had told us the same, and we didn't bother to follow their wisdom. We knew we could scare the bejeezus out of some old biddy, and we did it because we could. On top of that, we tried to hide from everyone. Then, when I was discovered, I lied about it. The top of the toppings is that I relished doing it.

WE ARE ALL CRACKED EIKONS

If there is anything the *post*modern generation is teaching us it is this: humans are not all they're cracked up to be. Which (ironically) means that humans are cracked, and the crack winds, like the Mighty Mississippi, right through the middle of the country of our heart.

My students don't care for sappy, sentimental love stories, and they don't think every politician can be trusted, and they don't believe everything they see on TV or read in newspapers. In other words, they know there are lots of agendas at work in this world and that agendas need to be seen for what they are. Instead of respectability or sociability, this generation values *authenticity*. *Star Wars* and *The Harry Potter* novels tell stories of *both* good and evil, and we like them (by the millions). If we have to follow the story all the way to the bottom, we will.

Embracing Grace

This generation has seen the public trials of celebrities, the moral collapse of pastors and priests, the exposure of a President's folly and his lies about it, the explosion of a spacecraft in the sky as they watched it live on TV in school with friends, the spread of AIDS and its chaser, death, to terrifying numbers, the intentional collision of airplanes into iconic symbols of the West with humans blowing themselves up in order to send a message, the brutalities of dictators, and the seemingly endless reporting about bloodshed in the Middle East. This generation has also been taught that our resources are fading. This generation knows. I wonder sometimes if maybe it knows too much.

But, it knows.

It knows humans are cracked Eikons and therefore this generation will not settle for smiley-faced yellow circles with upbeat ideas about a downbeat world. It knows, and it wants an authentic story that tells us what we know. This generation may want a story with hope all over it, but it won't settle for a testament of hope until it hears the truth about humans.

There is something wrong with humans, with every human we observe, and we all know it: like the story of the heartless man in England who, when he found a list of e-mail addresses for those who were searching for missing persons in South Asia after the indescribable impacts of the 2004 tsunami, wrote out fraudulent death notices and sent them to the families. How, we ask ourselves, could someone be so heartless? What, we ask ourselves, is humane about humanity?

This generation is entitled to ask *if* humans really are Eikons of *God*.

Most of us put up with this strange concoction of both goodness and badness in humans. Some turn cynical, like H. L. Mencken, that famous bird-dog hunter for human foibles who made Mark Twain's satires look Pollyanaish. In fact, Mencken blames it all on God (or on what people said about God): "All the errors and incompetencies of the Creator reach their climax in man." He responds to the claim that all humans have a soul, that it makes them superior to animals, and that it makes them aware of God. "Well, consider the colossal failure of the device. If we assume that man actually does resemble God, then we are forced into the impossible theory that God is a coward, an idiot and a bounder." A flashing, final cynical flourish: "The only practical effort of having a soul is that it fills man with [self-centered] vanities—in brief, with cocky and preposterous superstitions."

Mencken was cynical, but there were reasons for his being so. If credibility searches down the road of authenticity, then an authentic gospel will tell the authentic story of the human condition. It will include stories of both Mister Rogers and child abusers, both Mother Teresa and heartless exploiters, both Billy Graham and disgraced televangelists, both ordinary good folk and ordinary bad folk.

Why are humans this way? I invite you to consider the story of the cracked Eikon.

THE DAY THE EIKON CRACKED

Adam and Eve (read: humans) disobeyed the Creator God thinking they could find goodness and wisdom apart from God's good provisions. Adam and Eve were Eikons but they weren't (yet) perfect. They were immature, created to journey into union with God and communion with others, and they took care of God's good world. In their immaturity they were given a singular test.

According to the second chapter of Genesis, the good God, who turned the tohu va-bohu into a beautiful, orderly creation, with humans reflecting God to the entire created order, gave them (actually, "him" for he had given this commandment to Adam) one special prohibition: "You may freely eat of every tree of the garden; but of the tree of the knowledge of good and evil you shall not eat." Adam stored this in his heart, but at some point, perhaps during one of their evening walks when they were displaying God's glory to the rest of creation, he informed Eve of this prohibition. She, too, stored it in her heart.

Then one day, when Adam was doing some creative work of his own (or whatever he was doing before the plot thickened), Eve went nose to nose with the serpent, and the rest is the history we (sometimes generously) call civilization. Eve fell into the hands of the serpent, and Adam, looking like a dunce, fell as well, and they both ate the fruit they were told not to eat. When God inquired into the matter, they started pointing fingers in all directions. Adam: "The woman whom YOU gave to be with me," SHE is to blame. This was a lie, of course, but the situation demanded it. Refusing responsibility and pointing fingers has been with us ever since.

Booth Tarkington, who created marvelous Huck Finn-like characters in his Penrod books, got to the heart of the human condition in an episode after Penrod and his friend Sam created some mischief. Of them he said that "Penrod and Sam were not 'bad'; they were never that. They were something which was not their fault; they were *historic.*" I'm guessing Tarkington was laying blame on original sin or human solidarity, but the point is the same: humans often scribble the word "history" or "solidarity" in the sand to explain away the problem. For all our differences, we are all the same. We are cracked Eikons: Penrod and Sam, you and I, Adam and Eve.

Suddenly, all around Adam and Eve, the sound of the tohu va-bohu could be heard once again, a sound they had never heard. Here was a sound, like the rolling reminders of the ocean's presence for those who live on the shore, that would never go away. Afraid for their lives, they hid from God, behind a tree.

The Eikon of God cracked and its glory quickly faded. Why? Because what was designed for one purpose started to unravel. Arms that Adam and Eve previously used for an embrace were now being used to push God and others away. The heart no longer yearned for God, the soul clothed itself with mortality, the mind became disordered and could no longer make clear sense of the world in which it lived, the search for sanity began, the body no longer contained itself, the will lost control, and the sweet communion of Adam and Eve stretched into a weak connection. Union with God was weakened, communion with others was twisted, life became mortal, and the glory faded.

In short, the tohu va-bohu entered into the Eikon and it was as confused as the baby seal we recently saw, just after its birth, suddenly stranded by its mother on the shore as the mother sought food and the baby wondered what this world was all about. Confused about what had happened and fearful of what would happen next, both Adam and Eve sought cover from God. The Eikons suddenly discovered that they were lost in their own story, on the path of their own journey toward perfect union and communion. The Fall, or what I am calling the cracking of the Eikon as the Eastern Orthodox theologian Auxentios states it, "was not a departure from an originally static and perfect nature; it was the interruption—the cessation of a priceless process." They were on their way and they got lost.

The gospel tells us that we are all, more or less, lost. Searching, yes, but still at times confused about where to go and to whom to turn. I can think of no better example of a lost seeker than Alexander Cruden.

ALEXANDER THE CORRECTOR

When I was in high school and got serious about Bible study, my father taught me how to use *Young's Analytical Concordance* to the Bible. On occasion I would hear someone mention that instead of *Young's* they had used *Cruden's Complete Concordance to the Bible*. Alexander Cruden, born in 1699 into a pious Presbyterian family in Aberdeen, Scotland, was both weak and intelligent and both a consummate bungler and a devoted Bible student. An Eikon is designed for relationships with God and others, but Cruden was cracked right down the middle—sensitive in his relationship with God and insensitive in his relationships with others.

The details are now lost under the haze of cover-up and discretion. Somehow Cruden managed to fall in love, and he did something—no one knows what he did—with Thomas Blackwell's daughter and it landed him in Tolbooth, an institution for the mentally ill. Some believe this "relationship" was actually an incestuous relationship between the Blackwells' daughter and son issuing into a child that was blamed on Alexander Cruden to save the family name. Others aren't so sure. Was he guilty of a crime? We don't know. What we do know is that he was involved in three foolish but undamaging infelicitous attempts with women and four confinements in Tolbooth, and that he appointed himself "Alexander the Corrector" (of the nation's morals).

What we also know is that amidst all this swirling nonsense of one human's falling into the designs of another, Alexander Cruden did plenty of good: he managed to find time, after his long and mentally draining days of being a page corrector for publishers, to spend hours tediously compiling columns of every word in the Bible and noting the reference to each verse where that word occurred. It took him twelve years, but he eventually presented to the Queen a complete concordance to the Bible, the first ever. *Cruden's Concordance* has been in print for 250 years, and it was the one on which countless pastors relied when preparing sermons, and the one many faithful Bible readers of the Church consulted when they needed to know where a given word might be found. His legacy in the Church is permanent.

Cruden managed to bring glory to God because he was vulnerable to the cycle of grace. Later in his life, Alexander devoted himself to liberating unjustly accused people from imprisonment. He became a pastor to those who were in prison and spent his money feeding them and tending to their needs. Historians of prison systems know that Cruden was well ahead of his time in fighting for prison reform and for a more equitable evaluation before persons could be committed to what was then called "madhouses."

In the cracks of Cruden's life God made flowers grow.

Cruden illustrates the mess Adam and Eve got us into—the mess of being cracked. Nothing works perfectly: our relationships are sometimes good and sometimes bad; we do good things and we do bad things. The Bible calls our "crackedness" *sin*. But we can understand this term only if we begin at the beginning, recognizing that God designed humans for relationships with God and others, for the good of others and the world. The gospel that unleashes the cycle of grace gives us as much insight into the meaning of "sin" as it does into the meaning of grace.

THE CRACKS ARE RELATIONAL

Theological textbooks will tell you that sin is "any failure to perform the moral law of God in act, attitude, or nature." This definition is right but it isn't right enough. Breaking

God's good laws is surely sin, as the act of Adam and Eve to eat the fruit is sin. But, sin is more than this and deeper than this. Such a definition suggests that sin is inherently a legal issue, and when we define sin like this it becomes impersonal because law is impersonal. The reason such a textbook definition is not right enough is that it depersonalizes and de-relationalizes sin. The "genius" of sin is that it is first and foremost about one's relationship to God and others. Sin is a relational issue and as such transcends the legal issue. Infidelity is more than an offense of some contractual agreement; infidelity is the disruption or even destruction of a relationship.

Notice how Jesus teaches a relational view of sin. When the rich man comes to Jesus and asks him how he might inherit eternal life, Jesus reminds him of the Ten Commandments and sets up a legal situation. The Ten Commandments contain two kinds of laws: the First Table is about obeying God, and the Second Table is about treating others properly. But Jesus does not see the Ten Commandments as a set of laws. After mentioning the Second Table to the rich man, Jesus adds, "and love your neighbor as yourself." But this commandment is from Leviticus and is not one of the Ten Commandments. Why does Jesus suddenly quote Leviticus? Because he wants the rich man to understand that the commandments are relational: some are about loving God and some are about loving others.

If they are reduced to legal issues, they are misunderstood. For Jesus, the Law itself is not a comprehensive collection of laws such as one finds in tax guidelines that we are expected to read and follow. No, the Ten Commandments contain specific instances of the two governing relationships in life: loving God and loving others.

The implication of this teaching of Jesus for understanding sin is revolutionary: sin is clearly the breaking of a law, but more deeply it is a violation of loving God or others. In short, to continue with our image, the cracks in the Eikon are relational cracks.

Because the term "relational" is so broad and encompassing, we can understand why many today describe sin using terms like corruption and perversion and pollution and disintegration. These are accurate images for what happens when humans go their own way, when they run from God east of Eden or when they turn against their brother, as Cain did to Abel, or when they ruin the fields and the plains and the rivers, or when they destroy social networks and relationships. Sin corrupts relationships, it perverts relationships, it pollutes relationships, and it disintegrates relationships.

So, I agree with the many today who want the word "sin" back in the discussion, but the only way to do so is to give it its full biblical import: it is anything that breaks union with God or communion with others, anything that is unloving,

Embracing Grace

and anything that wants to establish any of these breaks of union as an earthly system. Sin encompasses much more than just breaking some legal code.

The theologian Cornelius Plantinga puts the whole discussion in perspective in the following terms: "Sin is disruption of created harmony and then resistance to divine restoration of that harmony." And, "God is for shalom and *therefore* against sin. . . . Sin is culpable shalom-breaking." He concludes, "In sum, shalom is God's design for creation and redemption; sin is blamable human vandalism of these great realities and therefore an affront to their architect and builder." If *Shalom* is another term for the kingdom of God Jesus came to establish, then sin is anything that impedes the kingdom of God.

Sin is so encompassing, we might say that it is *hyper-*relational.

5

THE EPIC
OF THE EIKON

ONLY THE ENDING OF A STORY MAKES THE BEGINNING CLEAR. Charles Dickens's *A Christmas Carol* begins with Ebenezer Scrooge's being both cheap and a creep, but in learning that his compass is pointing at doom, Scrooge enters what can only be called the generosity of grace. Compare this to the cult classic *Grease*. Sandy, played by Olivia Newton-John, is transformed from a long-dress-wearing goody two-shoes, into a brassy, bright-red-lipstick-wearing woman of the world stuffed into skin-tight black clothes. The innocence of conformity turns to the independence of counterculture. Millions have read Dan Brown's *The DaVinci Code,* and I did too. It was the ending of that book, apart from the historical howlers, that disturbed me most: worship of the divine goddess turns out to be the direction of the whole novel. Orthodoxy morphs into oppression.

Endings explain beginnings.

What we learn about God's Ending, Eternity, may tell us more about life in the Now than life in Eternity. There is an unbreakable connection between Eden and Eternity, between Genesis and Revelation, between The Beginning and The Ending.

That Ending is the subject of the last book in the Bible, the Revelation to St. John.

WHAT DOES REVELATION TELL US ABOUT ETERNITY?

Revelation is a story more bizarre than Maurice Sendak's *Where the Wild Things Are,* more graphic than Mel Gibson's *The Passion of the Christ,* and more satisfying than Jimmy Stewart's *It's a Wonderful Life.* Revelation, the most political book in the entire Bible, is the story of right finally being right and wrong finally being wrong, the story that gives back the Father, Son, and Holy Spirit their rightful due. This is why God is smack-dab in the middle. And in setting out the ordered universe of the End, Revelation gives up some of the mysteries of the Story of the End for us to consider.

First, the Ending comes with a battle. Chapter thirteen tells us that the dragon *stood* on the shore of the sea waiting for the evil beast to emerge from the chaotic sea. Then, one chapter later it tells us that the Lamb *stood* on Mount Zion awaiting the victorious saints of God. The sea locks horns with Mount Zion. The battle of the ages. The difference cannot be more graphic: like one of Homer's epics or a *Star Wars* movie, the world is split between those who pursue evil, who emerge from the sea, and those who pursue the kingdom of God, who stand with the Lamb on Zion. Death may be the last enemy that emerges from the sea, but it does not have the last word. The last word is Life with the Lamb on Zion.

Second, the Ending flows from life now. Eternity seems to begin with a millennial reign on earth lasting 1000 years, climaxing when the New Jerusalem and New Earth descend. Some interpret both millennium and New Jerusalem/New Earth literally—a real 1000 years of peace on earth and a physical Jerusalem and a new earth descending. Other Christian readers understand all of this as symbols of something "more," the 1000 years as the Church age and New Jerusalem as eternity. Imagery is never easy to interpret, and I'll not even begin to try to resolve these debates here. What is resolved is that the End perfects the earthly. But, if the End can be described as a New Jerusalem, we can only imagine that it will be a robust, complete society where the cycle of grace runs perfectly and where humans carry on their normal but enhanced gifts and abilities.

Third, Jesus Christ is the central figure of the Ending. He is, to use the mixed imagery of the author, King and Lamb and temple and light and (once again) King. Each of the following lines from chapters 1, 5, 21, and 11 needs to be read:

John to the seven churches that are in Asia: Grace to you and peace from him who is and who was and who is to come, and from the seven spirits who are before his throne, and from Jesus Christ, the faithful witness, the firstborn of the dead, and the ruler of the kings of the earth. To him who loves us and freed us from our sins by his blood . . .

They sing a new song: "You are worthy to take the scroll and to open its seals, for you were slaughtered and by your blood you ransomed for God saints from every tribe and language and people and nation; you have made them to be a kingdom and priests serving our God, and they will reign on earth."

I saw no temple in the city, for its temple is the Lord God the Almighty and the Lamb. And the city has no need of sun or moon to shine on it, for the glory of God is its light, and its lamp is the Lamb.

The kingdom of the world has become the kingdom of our Lord and of his Messiah, and he will reign forever and ever.

Fourth, the humans in the Ending are the good people of God. On the twelve gates were the names of the twelve tribes of Israel, and on the twelve foundations were written the names of the twelve apostles (21:12-13). The people of God is the one people of God, beginning with Abraham and Israel and climaxing in the people of Jesus Christ, the Church.

Finally, at the center of the Ending is human worship and praise to God and the Lamb. To "worship" God means more than to fold our hands, bow our heads, and endlessly sing uplifting hymns in an assembly of Christians plopped down on pews while heavenly harpists orchestrate yet one more rendition of "My Jesus I Love Thee." Worship, according to chapter twelve of Romans, is offering our bodies—that is, all we are—as a living and holy and acceptable sacrifice. Worship, then, is a life lived as it is meant to be lived: for the good of others and the world.

To synthesize this, there are two deep dimensions to the Ending. Humans will be in union with God and in communion with others, for the good of others and the entire created order. It is Eden all over again, only better. Eternity is the unleashing of the cycle of embracing grace.

Which means that Eternity is absorption into the perichoresis of God and perfect communion with others.

THE WHEEL

One might liken Eternity to a wheel and the spokes of that wheel. Each person may be likened to a small ring that slides up and down on a spoke. When Adam and Eve sinned and set the world spinning into chaos again, each of us was thrust by centrifugal forces from the very presence of God to the "rim" of the wheel (cast from Eden). In earthly life, persons find themselves located at the rim of the wheel at a maximum distance from both God and others. The gospel for Now is God gloriously drawing us back with centripetal forces into God's love. As each person comes closer to God (sliding down the spoke) each person also comes closer to others. Maybe we should call this wheel illustration the "geography of the gospel"—and map our own location.

If Eternity is the perfection of our union with God and communion with others, we are on that glorious descent even now. Sometimes we snatch a glimpse of what it will be like and find ourselves transfixed into speechlessness as we stand between Now and Eternity.

Off and on in my life I have read mystics, people like St. John of the Cross and St. Francis, or even more modern mystics like Evelyn Underhill, Frank Laubach, and Thomas Merton. I read the mystics because of an experience I had in high school. During a particularly intense period of spiritual formation, when things were suddenly coming together for me, I had a habit before going to sleep of kneeling at my bed simply to give thanks to God for my day. On one occasion, as I began to pray, I sensed in my dark room that I was being surrounded from above by a brilliant, warm light. I sensed that I was becoming unusually heavy. I sensed an incredible union with God in my communication, but I was also suddenly incapable of speaking—all I could do was bask in this glorious light and (what I believed to be) the presence of God's Spirit. It was an experience of a dangerous kind of safe, or a safe kind of danger. I don't know how long the experience of glimpsing what was Beyond lasted, but when I opened my eyes I saw the hues of my bedcover and felt my sore knees, and before long (like the Pevensie children in the Narnian tales), I fell out of the wardrobe into my own room and all was normal again.

This kind of ecstatic experience of union with God is not unusual for Christian mystics. I believe that Eternity will be an uninterrupted flow of such ecstatic union with God. We will be, in our very natures, blended into the presence of God while maintaining our identity. To repeat a previously used theological term, we will enter into the perichoresis.

HEAVENLY COMMUNE

Having related how we will be united with God in perfect union, let me emphasize again the communal nature of

Embracing Grace

Eternity. In Revelation, or any other images of Eternity in the Bible, we do not find humans camping out in isolation from one another. Just the opposite is the case: the quarters of Eternity seem, like a church camp, a tad cramped and simple. C. S. Lewis, in *The Great Divorce,* describes hell as a place where diminished humans are constantly in search of distance between themselves and others. Eternity, in contrast, is a place where humans will seek proximity to one another because in that proximity they come to know God and themselves.

Another way of saying this is that the Ending is the kingdom: when Eikons are who they are meant to be, when husbands and wives love one another utterly, when moms and dads love their children utterly, when children love their parents utterly, and when each person—young and old, diverse as the rainbow, sized as differently as they are—loves God, the other, and the world—utterly. When bus drivers love commuters utterly, when commuting drivers love other commuting drivers utterly, when bosses love employees utterly and when employees love bosses utterly and when professors love administrators and administrators love professors utterly. There will be no law courts, because humans will transcend justice with love; there will be no locks because humans will own what they need and rejoice in what others own . . . and on and on in the perichoretic circle of Eternal Light. Not a monotonous dance but one full of twists and turns and surprises and joys, like a journey into an endlessly new country where around every corner is something wondrous and spectacular.

ETERNITY AND THE GOSPEL NOW

If we begin with this Ending to the story, we gain a new glimpse of Now.

Learning about the End does not permit us to escape from the present, and if we are seeking an escape we misunderstand that End. The End is the perfected drama of what is to occur here and now. We know the End so we can live Now.

Robert Webber, who stirred a generation of students (and administrators) at Wheaton College, expresses the demand of the current generation for a Church that lives up to its End: "The church," he says, "does not *have* an eschatology, it *is* an eschatological people." One of his students and now the pastor of a burgeoning church, Rob Bell, puts it like this: "When we choose God's vision of who we are, we are living as God made us to live. We are living in the flow of how we are going to live forever. This," he emphasizes, "is the life of heaven, here and now. . . . As we live this way, heaven comes here. To this place, this world, the one we're living in."

Jesus prayed for the kingdom to come to earth as it was in heaven—now. That is why we have St. John's book called Revelation.

Embracing Grace

AUTHORS OF THE END

In the history of the Church no two books have had more enduring impact on Christians' learning to live in the Now in the light of the End than John's Bunyan's *Pilgrim's Progress* and Dante's brilliant *Divine Comedy—The Inferno*. Dante begins with these famous words:

> When I had journeyed half of our life's way,
> I found myself within a shadowed forest,
> for I had lost the path that does not stray.

Bunyan, much more interested in fleeing the worldliness of the world, starts out as follows:

> As I walked through the wilderness of this world, I lighted on a certain place where there was a Den, and I lay down there to sleep. As I slept, I dreamed a dream.
>
> Behold, I saw a man clothed with rags, standing with his face looking away from his own house, a Book in his hand, and a great burden on his back. As I looked, he opened the Book, and read in it, and as he read, he wept and trembled. Not being able to contain himself any longer, he began to weep, saying, "What shall I do?"

For Dante, an experience of the inferno and the progress through purgatory and into paradise was a moral mirror of what was happening in central Italy in the thirteen and fourteenth centuries. If one saw oneself, or what could become of oneself in his *Comedy*, then the better part of wisdom was to do something about it. His descriptions of what happens in inferno have evoked many to give their life to God.

Bunyan intended the same. Traveling with person after person, finding place after place, and encountering worry after worry, the central character, Christian, vigilantly turns from worldly options and plods the path from the City of Destruction until he crosses the river into the Celestial City, where he finds himself in the presence of God.

Many are unnerved by the amount of judgment, not to say graphic imagery, in these two classic books, but the overall impact can be sought elsewhere: that humans are invited to live Now in light of the End.

Again, this presents an old problem. Many focus so much on heaven that life here doesn't seem to matter. Both Bunyan and (to a lesser degree) Dante can foster such an orientation. But the Story of the End turns the Story of the Now into our future epic. I like what Marilynne Robinson, in her novel *Gilead,* says about keeping the earthly and the heavenly in balance. When Pastor John Ames, the main character, watches his young wife and their son blowing bubbles to a cat's delight outside his window, John also sees the bubbles float into the heavens: "You two," he muses, "were too intent on the cat to see the celestial consequences of your worldly endeavors." Marilynne Robinson adds to this theme later when John says this: "And I can't believe that, when we have all been changed and put on incorruptibility, we will forget our fantastic condition of mortality and impermanence, the great bright dream of procreating and perishing that meant the whole world to us. In eternity this world will be Troy, I believe, and all that has passed here will be the epic of the universe, the ballad they sing in the streets. Because I don't imagine any reality putting this one in the shade entirely, and I think piety forbids me to try."

6

PAGE AFTER PAGE

GOD DESIGNED THE GOSPEL FOR *US*.

God designs the gospel for more than *my* goodness and *my* sin and *my* redemption and *my* liberation and *my* experience and *my* chance to go to heaven when *I* die. The gospel is about *us* before it is about *me*. My own *I* is in the *Us*, and a gospel of *I* without an *Us* is a gospel about *me*. I'm glad the gospel is for *me* but it is about more than me.

The cycle of grace is shaped for Eikons instead of *individualists*. Because the gospel begins with God creating us and because being God's special creation is all about being relationally shaped, the gospel itself is designed to restore us *both* with God *and* with others. Again, let us go to the End to see what it means for us to say that the gospel is community-shaped.

Notice these beautiful and climactic words from the twenty-first chapter of Revelation, a description of what occurs when both Jerusalem and the earth are perfectly restored and when God comes to dwell among his people:

> And I heard a loud voice from the throne saying,
> "See, the home of God is among mortals.
> He will dwell with them as their God;
> they will be his peoples,
> and God himself will be with them."

This evocative language of God's dwelling with us and our being a community is the language of the covenant from Exodus and Leviticus. The twenty-ninth chapter of Exodus says this of God: "I will dwell among the Israelites, and I will be their God." And the twenty-sixth chapter of Leviticus says of God: "I will place my dwelling in your midst. . . . And I will walk among you, and will be your God, and you shall be my people." From the beginning, God's design was to dwell among us and to create a community for us.

This fundamental principle leads to the heart of the gospel: it is the work of God, *in the context of a community,* to restore us to union with God and communion for the good of others and the world.

EIKONS ARE DESIGNED
FOR COMMUNITY

The thickest barricade to the gospel is Individualism. Many speak about selfishness and pride, and I agree that these interfere with the cycle of grace, but nothing interferes with the flow of gospel grace more than Individualism. Individualism is an intentional march away from Eden, away from God and away from others. When the gospel is packaged as attractive to individuals instead of a community, the problem is only compounded.

The gospel, you will recall, is the work of the triune, inter-personal God—a God in whom community is essence. And humans are made in God's Eikon with a relationally pointed compass. If the direction of this gospel compass is union with God and communion with others, then we can be "re-unioned" with God and "re-communioned" with others. Which means this—and I know this may sound edgy to some: the gospel is designed to create community out of individualists.

Adam, God noticed, was alone and it was not good.

FROM ADAM AND EVE
TO ABRAHAM

There are only a few verses in the Bible, less than fifteen to be exact (Gen. 2: 4–17), when a human existed solely as an individual, and God's comment when he looked at

Embracing Grace

Adam on his own was that it was not good for Adam to be an individualist. From that moment on the rest of the Bible is about humans living more or less—and a lot of the time less—in community.

If we read from Genesis 3 to Genesis 12, we find two big ideas. First, God gives Adam's descendants an opportunity to figure out this cracked Eikon business, and they botch it. From Cain's murdering Abel to Noah's disgrace and Ham's (Noah's son) broadcasting of that disgrace and then to the unquenchable desire to make a name for themselves by constructing a tower to the heavens—we read of one disaster after another. That's the first idea. Adam lived a short while as an individualist, and we might say that from Genesis 3 to 12 humans tried an individualistic lifestyle. But, as God says, it is not good for humans to be alone.

The second idea from Genesis 3 to Genesis 12 is this: with Abraham, God makes a fresh start, and the design of that start is to form a community, wherein the purposes of God will be worked out properly. The rest of the Old Testament is about that community. In my English translation with small print and double columns, that makes for 1237 pages—the "story" of the community, the wisdom and prayer and proverbial literature of that community, and the prophets of that community. Over 1200 pages of small print about how that community fared—its ups and downs, and its ins and outs.

From Abraham on, God charts out a different journey, and it begins with God's deciding to *form a people*—a family, a tribe, a community, a nation, and a Church for all nations. This is why the gospel is about *us*.

IT TAKES A COMMUNITY TO TELL THE GOSPEL: "COME AND SEE"

This community is the gospel's best "embodiment" of its message; it is the community that proclaims the gospel the most clearly. One of the Church's best preachers and one of her deepest influences is John Wesley, who lived from 1703 to 1791 and who preached thousands of sermons. Under the influence of three contemporaries, John and Charles Wesley, and George Whitefield, the gospel spread like a fire across much of Great Britain and the United States.

Not all were happy about the gospel Wesley was preaching. In 1740 a deist, Conyers Middleton (1683–1750), published a challenge to the Christian belief in miracles and called into question the integrity of the Christian gospel Wesley was preaching. Though scheduled to visit with a friend in Rotterdam, John Wesley delayed his trip twenty days so he could sort through Middleton's challenge and respond as clearly and charitably as possible. The result was an essay called "A Plain Account of Genuine Christianity" that demonstrates that for this revivalist the best evidence for the

Embracing Grace

Christian faith is the power of a transformed life as seen in a community of faith. The most enduring part of Wesley's response to Middleton was tucked away at the end of his response. After defining what can be called a genuine Christian and what can be called genuine Christianity, Wesley made a simple but potent appeal in eight words to Middleton and laid his gospel on the line with this: "Come and see what Christianity has done here." This from a man whose very livelihood was preaching, whose heart was on fire with the spoken and written word. But, for John Wesley the best defense of the gospel was the power of a community holding on snuggly as it rides into the cycle of grace itself.

This is precisely what the entire sweep of the biblical drama calls humans to do: come and see what God can do when he transforms cracked Eikons. Come and see, and you will find it in a community. The gospel finds its most articulate expression, as Jesus said in John 13, when his disciples love one another: "By this everyone will know that you are my disciples, if you have love for one another."

PAGE AFTER PAGE

God began the process of creating a community through a covenant with Abraham. Through Abraham, Moses, David and Jesus, God renewed and ramped up that original covenant promise to Abraham. From Abraham to Isaac to Jacob to Joseph in Egypt. From the liberation of Israel from Egypt to the wandering in the wilderness and to crossing the Jordan. From the building of Jerusalem under David and Solomon to the carting off of its people to Assyria and then later to Babylon and to their coming back to Jerusalem and starting all over again. This is the story of a community.

Page after page after page, some with lists of who begat whom and descriptions of buildings and laws about marriages and about what to eat and what not to eat and outlines for the temple. On some pages we read about prophets calling kings to account, and the people to shape up or else, and foreign kings to heed their words, and on others we read of kings calling the people to muster more faith, and we learn about wars with other nations and border disputes—and some of this doesn't make all that interesting a reading. We read psalm after psalm about David and his enemies and the people of God being happy when they see the nation prosper. And this can seem unimportant at times. But it is important, the way a newspaper is important in the morning.

Why? Because the earthly shape of God's community is the centerpiece of God's restoring work. Because the work of God is to restore each of us *in the context of a community* in the here and now. The history of Israel is not the failed attempt of a nation between two big moments in history—

between the Fall and the Cross. You tear the heart out of God's work on earth if you skip from the Fall to the Cross.

At each stage of the process in this history, God is working with *communities:* a family tribe (Abraham), an entire nation (Moses), a kingdom (David), and a universal Church (Jesus). With Jesus we run smack-dab into the middle of a term that makes this very clear: Jesus' mission was to bring the *kingdom,* and the kingdom is a community or a society wherein the will of God—what I call the Jesus Creed—is done. Humans are restored to God and to others, and they can be healed and sustained through pain as they are drawn into a community of faith.

Bobbi Peacock discovered the healing power of a community of faith in Minneapolis where she is participating in the gospel of embracing grace. Here are her words:

> Grieving over the death of a close friend and my husband asking for a divorce within a week of one another . . . the reality that I was going to be a single mom, going back to work to support myself and Ella, living with the pain, the guilt, the shame. Moving cross-country. Finding a job. Finding a place to live. Finding day care. Letting go of my daughter so that another woman may care for her. Broken heart. Broken dreams. I prayed and prayed and prayed. Night and day. Silently. Out loud.

And after detailing some good things in her life, Bobbi says:

> I haven't told anyone at the Porch [the church's name] how instrumental they've been to me in recovering from my divorce and grief of my loss . . . but I am grateful for each and every one of you.
>
> God bless you all!!! Thank you for accepting me and being my friend.

Bobbi stands in line with others who witness to the power of the gospel when it is performed by a community.

When the poets Donald Hall and Jane Kenyon moved from Ann Arbor, Michigan, to the family farm in Eagle Pond, New Hampshire, to see if they could make a living simply on their writing, they were confronted with the decision about church. Here are Donald's words: "The first Sunday we were alone together, I said that maybe we ought to go to church. . . . We went, and heard a sermon. . . . Jack Jensen quoted 'Rilke the German poet,' which didn't diminish our attention. What most ensnared us was not references to Rilke or theology, but the community of the church." This community, which was to play a central role in the lives of Donald and Jane, especially when Donald fought his way through cancer and when Jane tragically lost her battle with cancer, is what attracted them to the church when they moved to New Hampshire.

Embracing Grace

THE GOSPEL
AND THE COMMUNITY

The Church is not a collection of random individuals who happen each to believe in Jesus Christ, who happen to be working out "their own salvation," who happen to be living in proximity to one another, who happen to enjoy the same preachers and musicians and liturgy, and who happen to affirm the same doctrinal convictions. The Church is a community of faith wherein humans are "re-communioned" to one another.

Page after page we read about this community.

7

A MISSIONAL GOSPEL

WE BEGIN WITH OUR DEFINITION OF THE GOSPEL to this point: the gospel is the work of God, in the context of a community, to restore Eikons to union with God and communion with others, for the good of others and the world. There is more to come, but for now there are four major elements in this definition:

The source: it is God's work.
The place: in the context of a community.
The purpose: to restore us to God and others.
The mission: for the good of others and the world.

This was the gospel of Jesus. The central creed in life for Judaism, which Jesus slightly amended, was this:

Hear O Israel, the Lord our God. The Lord is One. Love the Lord your God with all your heart, with all your soul, with all your mind, and with all your strength.

To which Jesus added:

And the second is this: Love your neighbor as yourself. There is no commandment greater than these.

(author's translations)

What Jesus is calling for in the *Jesus Creed*, for us to love God and others, is the *purpose* of the gospel. God restores us so we will become loving. Loving God with heart, soul, and mind is fairly easy to grasp, but what might it mean for us to love God "with all our *strength*"? This expression, I am suggesting, opens up the opportunity for us to consider the *mission* of the gospel.

The word "strength," *moedeka* in Hebrew, means more than physical strength and more than just our body. It is not intended to describe weightlifters or the crisp cuts of the young. Instead, "strength" refers to our "externalities," to our "resources," to what we do in the physical world that can be seen, touched, smelled, and tasted. When we read "with all your strength," instead of thinking of fitness shows on TV we should think of everything we see and touch and taste in the world.

In other words, to love God "with all your strength" means that we are to love God with everything we do, with everything we say, with everything we touch, with everything we smell, with everything we eat or choose not to eat, with everything we buy and don't buy, with everything we own, with everything we make, with every cultural establishment, with every social institution and with every global structure . . . . and on and on.

And, because it concerns how we love the whole created order, the gospel is a holistic work of God. The gospel unleashes a cycle of grace that is extended *to the entire created order*. If God embraces the entire created order in his plan, then we too are invited to join him.

WHEN CRACKED EIKONS
GET TOGETHER

Loving God with all our strength tackles one of our world's deepest issues. When cracked Eikons get together they do cracked things together. Which means that humans create systemic problems, systemic violence, and systemic evil. Systemic evil describes any system or institution or governmental structure or local business policy that is contrary to God's will and that oppresses people and creates a cycle of injustice. Systemic evil is a label for exploiting the environment and the poor, for both racism and laws that privilege one class over another.

The gospel is designed to end systemic evil and to establish the kingdom.

But cracked Eikons create systemic evil when they abuse children; they create systemic evil in their local communities when they swing deals behind closed doors; they create systemic evil when governments block justice to certain groups and create privileges for others; they create systemic evil when they use schools as platforms to brainwash children into believing and acting upon blatant lies; they create systemic evil when they refuse to follow environmentally sensitive laws. Instead of creating order out of the tohu va-bohu, humans sometimes create tohu va-bohu out of order.

Again, let this be said: the gospel is designed to end systemic violence and to establish the kingdom, because the gospel is a holistic work of God.

Kingdom people care about systemic evil because God cares about the entire created order. The apostle Paul knew the magnitude of the kingdom vision in dismantling systemic evil and told the Christians at Ephesus, in chapter six of his letter to them, that "our struggle is not against enemies of blood and flesh, but against the rulers, against the authorities, against the cosmic powers of this present darkness, against the spiritual forces of evil in the heavenly places."

Jesus knew systemic evil from his own experience. His family fled to Egypt for fear of Jesus' being put to death; his mother was considered an adulteress, and that meant that Jesus, her son, was considered an illegitimate child, bringing some levels of ostracism for both of them; his cousin, the prophet John the Baptist, was put to death by Roman leadership. Jesus was accused of all sorts of things, but he continually sat at table with everyone, and, after praying, passed to each person at the table a bowlful of food from his warm pot of grace.

This is why Jesus spoke about God's work as the kingdom of God.

A HOLISTIC GOSPEL

Because the tohu va-bohu has penetrated into the very fabric of society, state, and culture, the gospel is holistic. It is for every part of each person—heart, soul, mind, and strength—and it is for every part of the whole world—the economical, political, legal, and cultural realms. It is for *all of us* in the sense of each one of us and every part of us.

Ronald Sider, who has labored tirelessly for three generations for this gospel, says that a holistic gospel:

• teaches a ministry that integrates discipleship, evangelism, and social action, and works toward both spiritual and social transformation.

• supports a spectrum of social action that includes charity, compassion, community development, public policy, and justice advocacy, addressing both individual and systemic sources of human problems.

• sees ministry as fundamentally relational, seeking to develop long-term relationships with ministry recipients and welcoming them into church fellowship.

• views mission as both local and global in scope.

GOD'S EMBRACE OF THE WORLD

Sometimes we are tempted to reduce the gospel to individuals' being reconciled to God personally or even to God forming our own special community. But the work of God is more than individual redemption, and it does not stop at community formation. God's work is *with* the whole world and *for* the whole world. kingdoms, after all, don't stop with the individual or with communities.

Many have pointed to passages in the Bible where God seems to have the whole world in mind, passages like the first two chapters of Genesis or a psalm or two where the psalmist suddenly erupts into how great God is because of what can be seen in the created order, but none expresses it any better than the apostle Paul's observations in the eighth chapter of Romans:

> I consider that the sufferings of this present time are not worth comparing with the glory about to be revealed to us. For the creation waits with eager longing for the revealing

of the children of God; for the creation was subjected to futility, not of its own will but by the will of the one who subjected it, in hope that the creation itself will be set free from its bondage to decay and will obtain the freedom of the glory of the children of God. We know that the whole creation has been groaning in labor pains until now; and not only the creation, but we ourselves, who have the first fruits of the Spirit, groan inwardly while we wait for adoption, the redemption of our bodies.

The gospel Paul preached was cosmic, and he longed for the day when *"creation itself* will be set from its bondage to decay." Creation, it should be observed, longs for humans to be restored to God and to others because it knows that only then will it be what God made it to be.

God's loving arms are around the globe, around adults and trees and mountains, children and rivers and birds, moms and dads and lions and elephants, little poor children and adult poor people and cultures and ethnicities, and governments and art shows and building projects. Around golf courses and sweat shops, around country clubs and inner-city slums, around high-rise penthouses and humans in ghettos.

Over the centuries the Church has suffered when it has permitted itself to offer a tiny gospel to individual souls so they could dwell in Bunyan's Celestial City or Dante's Paradise or C. S. Lewis's Narnia. It suffers when it treats humans as souls made for eternity instead of whole persons made for now and eternity. But, there are fresh winds blowing throughout the Christian world, brought on in part by the AIDS crisis and by the attention given to massive poverty and by the realization of the systemic evil connected with racism and international tensions and bloodshed.

These new winds are suggesting that churches start in their own backyards to set a holistic gospel loose at the grassroots level. Churches are beginning to establish neighborhood groups for neighborly reasons: to know the neighbors, to learn names, to sit over coffee or to have a picnic or to talk to one another. Out of such neighborliness needs are mentioned, and before long nameless houses on the street become homes where living, breathing needs are discovered. Neighborhoods in which people listen to one another create communities, and communities create a world where God would be quite happy to dwell among us.

LOOKING, LISTENING, LEARNING, AND LINKING: THE PRINCIPLES OF MISSIONAL COMMUNITIES

The word favored for this new focus is *missional*. Missional communities of faith seek to perform a holistic gospel, and they are found among Protestants, Roman Catholics, and the Eastern Orthodox. There are four characteristics of such communities of faith: these Christians *look* out and see people and the world, they *listen* to the pain of people and the groanings of the world, they *learn* what they can do, and they *link* themselves to those local needs for the good of others and the world. Missional communities incarnate a holistic gospel. Anything less is not gospel.

This sort of linking is as varied as it is intentional: if we look, listen, and learn there will be a link for each of us—both to the created world and to our societies. There are many opportunities, and it is encouraging to see so many at work.

LINKING TO CREATION

Adam and Eve were instructed to govern the garden—to nurture it and to care for it. This concern for creation shows up throughout the Bible, not the least in the great Psalm 19, where we find the declaration of what I have experienced numerous times myself: "the heavens are telling the glory of God." Jesus' own words in Matthew, chapter ten, about God's critters the sparrows, expresses the same theme: "Yet not one of them will fall to the ground apart from your Father." It perhaps needs to be emphasized that linking to the created order joins alongside the direction of God's gospel work.

As Brian McLaren observes, "Maybe God allows each of us to join God in loving some special aspect of creation, from

Embracing Grace

weather to stars to dinosaurs to rocks to antique cars to song-birds to lions to electricity to wines to motorcycles to giant salamanders." The wisdom here of Wendell Berry is important. We need to begin locally. "If we could think locally, we would take far better care of things than we do now. The right local questions and answers will be the right global ones. The Amish question 'What will this do to our community?' tends toward the right answer for the world."

One who did begin locally has become synonymous with American naturalism. John Muir's passion for creation was so thorough that his name is connected to preserving our natural resources. This is why a redwood forest across San Francisco's Bay Bridge is named Muir Woods. Walking among these trees, some dating from Charlemagne's time, gives one a sense of a virginal world, untouched by commercial develop-ment. But, it takes humans like John Muir to care for redwood forests, humans who know they are created as Eikons and who as Eikons, are to "govern" God's good world. Caring for the world is one example of what it means to love God "with all your strength." Because of people like John Muir or Roger Tory Peterson, the famous ornithologist and bird artist, many of us today are concerned with our world—whether we are light or dark in our Green concerns. I am a bird watcher, and we donate some of our money to help preserve birds in danger of extinction, like the peregrine falcon. Just today when Kris and I were walking through a local preserve, Independence Grove, we spotted our first ever bobolink, dressed up as it was in its tuxedo-like plumage. Other people link to other parts of the created order, but we can each do something.

Recently, we were on Oregon's coastline when we saw a small crowd of people gathered around some cause of commotion. We walked over to find that a mother seal had just given birth to a baby seal, and she had returned to the ocean to do whatever seal mothers do when they go back into the ocean following a birth. It was a unique event for us, but what also impressed us was that the Oregonians knew what not to do, and they pointed it out when these Midwesterners thought getting close was a good thing. No, they knew to stay back at least fifty yards so as not to alienate the mother. Everyone knew this. They also knew that a person could get fined a small drawerfull of money if one got too close. Again, humans caring for the created world in their local world. A friend who was with us said, "I wish these people cared as much about the salmon." Therein lies another story, but I was impressed by yet another link to the created order. Humans, as Eikons of God, are given by their Creator the responsibility to govern this world—and if they don't, the world will be ravaged by humans who think "me first" and not "other creatures too" or "world too." I know others who protest eating certain kinds of meat because of the way such animals are raised or put to death—one more Christian concern with the world God has given us.

Christians who are linking into their world with a holistic gospel are not necessarily working only with global or monstrous problems—like AIDS or rainforests or injustices in war-torn countries. It is a mistake to think the only way to love people is to love people who have big problems—though I think all of us should participate in global issues as well. Genuine neighborliness listens and looks in one's own neighborhood, beginning next door and down the street and across the street, and learns and links right there in a local context. Neighborly love begins in one's home and with one's own neighbors and thus unleashes the cycle of grace into our society and even further into our world.

I sense that churches that do not respond to this challenge to link to the world with a holistic gospel will soon be left stranded on an island called "Irrelevant."

LINKING TO SOCIETY

There are many examples of churches that are linking to their society, like Redeemer Presbyterian Church in New York City, James Meeks's Salem Baptist in Chicago, the Mosaic Church of Los Angeles, St. Pius X Catholic Church of Beaumont, Texas, or the fifteen churches described so well in Ronald Sider's *Churches that Make a Difference*. These churches are compassionate, and their compassion moves them to action. They are churches committed to a holistic gospel—and they do so in the context of a vibrant community. (I do not want to claim some high ground here and suggest that only churches are doing this sort of work, for that is untrue. What I am saying is that a missional gospel is at work in many communities, and that the number of such churches is growing.)

A concern to link to one's society for the good of the world is rooted deeply in the pages of the Bible. Among the many passages one could consider, standing tall is Peter's first letter to the churches of Asia Minor. This letter was the first extensive Christian reflection on how Christians were to relate to their society because, as that first century continued along, Christians were beginning to realize they were in this world for the long haul. Notice these words from chapter two:

> Beloved, I urge you as aliens and exiles to abstain from the desires of the flesh that wage war against the soul. Conduct yourselves honorably among the Gentiles, so that, though they malign you as evildoers, they may see your honorable deeds and glorify God when he comes to judge. For the Lord's sake accept the authority of every human institution, whether of the emperor as supreme, or of governors, as sent by him to punish those who do wrong and to praise those who do right. For it is God's will that

Embracing Grace

by doing right you should silence the ignorance of the foolish. As servants of God, live as free people, yet do not use your freedom as a pretext for evil. Honor everyone. Love the family of believers. Fear God. Honor the emperor.

The Christians to whom Peter was writing were suffering persecution for their faith, and they needed advice from this wise and aging apostle. Instead of withdrawing from society, instead of throwing lightning bolts at the ills of society, Peter advised that they were to live as a family and a community of God, meaning they were to be persons of "honorable deeds," which involved civic responsibility, benevolent actions like erecting public buildings, and general care for the good of the public welfare.

There are many in the world today taking up this task of linking to society as a missional family of God. Some of the most notable examples are taking root in an urban landscape. Recently, Curtis DeYoung and three other writer-practitioners gave a challenge for suburban Christians to return to the urban context to make a difference. Their own story can be found in *United by Faith: The Multiracial Congregation as an Answer to the Problem of Race.* Their efforts are being copied in many places, not always with instant success, but with a genuine sense that all of God's people—red and yellow, black and white—ought to be united on Sunday, because the gospel is for all of us.

One such community is Reba Place Fellowship and Reba Place Church in Evanston, Illinois. As a missional community that is at the same time a story of restoring cracked Eikons Reba today continues to inspire others to imagine new ways to link to their local community with the cycle of grace. Reba is an intentional Christian community of about forty persons living in homes and apartments, and they have also purchased some commercial buildings for a variety of purposes. Sensing that consumerism and rampant individualism were damaging the witness of the gospel, in 1957 a group of Christians moved to Evanston to revitalize an older way of "doing gospel": by living in community for the good of the local community. Nearly five decades later Reba continues to work out its focus: "to extend the mission of Jesus by being a community of love and discipleship, and to nurture other such communities as God gives us grace." Hence, Reba Place fosters small groups, weekly meetings to discern God's voice together, and weekly potluck meals open to others. These potluck meals are a good place for those who are questing to find ways to link to their communities, to sit down and learn from practitioners.

At Reba Early Learning center more than fifty preschoolers are cared for; volunteers from Reba and other churches work hard to discover and maintain affordable housing for others; ASSETS helps others start up new businesses; The Clearing

Embracing Grace

is a ministry for disabled adults; Harvest provides low-cost health foods; the Pick provides free clothing; and the House of Manna finds and distributes recently outdated food. And, by the way, Reba Place is also a Christian church: fellowshiping together, praying together, learning Scriptures together, celebrating the Eucharist and preaching the gospel weekly—and seeking to embody the gospel holistically in its own particular community.

FOR THE GOOD OF OTHERS AND THE WORLD

Our invitation to love God "with all our strength" invites us to be missional communities of faith. It invites us to love God with everything we see and experience, everything we have and hear, and everything we establish and co-create with our Creator God. Restored Eikons care about the rivers as well as the cities that grow along them, about mountains as well as the tall buildings that imitate those mountains in the heart of our cities, and they care about environmental laws as well as laws governing human behavior. They know the gospel is to be both proclaimed and performed in a missional community.

The gospel, once again, is the work of God, in the context of a community, to restore Eikons to union with God and communion with others for the good of others *and the world.* All of this is gospel work.

8

STORIES OF THE
GOSPEL STORY

WE CONFESS THAT THE GOSPEL IS THE WORK OF GOD to restore us in the context of a community to God and to others for the good of others and the world. We need to pause once again to notice how big this claim is: it is something God does for us and to us, and the long-term direction of God's embrace, so we are claiming, will benefit *the whole world*. Somehow, we are suggesting, we are to be a "blessing" to the world.

Let's all admit something: the enormity of the task makes a much smaller gospel, one tailored for individuals, so much more attractive. It would be easier to promise forgiveness from sins and heaven when we die. But that is the one thing, Jesus tells us in his kingdom vision, that we cannot let happen. As followers of Jesus we are stuck with a big gospel with a big claim.

If the gospel is this big, we have to ask two mechanical questions: "What does the gospel actually do for us when it 'restores' us?" and "How does the restoration process actually work?" (This is actually a different question, but we'll get to that shortly.)

WHAT DOES THE GOSPEL DO FOR US?

The claim of the gospel is astounding. Embracing grace, so it is claimed, begins to resolve three fundamental questions about life that have surfaced from time to time in what has been said so far: the problem of suffering, the problem of sin, and the problem of systemic evil. Here are the claims the gospel makes for itself:

First, for the question about *suffering*, the gospel claims that Jesus Christ *absorbs suffering and pain* in his torturous death on the cross. One word in the Bible brings this home: "Immanuel," or "God with us." The gospel claims God is with us in our suffering by descending all the way down into the deepest of our deaths.

Second, for the question of human *sinfulness*, the gospel claims that God—Father, Son, Spirit—graciously embraces us, and that embrace *forgives us, restores us, enables us,* and *empowers us.*

And, third, for the question of a world awash in *systemic evil,* the gospel claims that Jesus Christ offers *an alternative community: the kingdom of God.*

These problems are our problems, and there is no gospel if there is no resolution to these problems.

We know that we are one second from fatal blows and one medical call away from torturous diseases and one chasm away from sin-issues and just as much a chasm away from moral perfection and (seemingly) centuries shy of the kingdom. But the gospel claims that God is both all-good and all-powerful, and that evil is something God has permitted into the world by creating such a thing as freedom. And, instead of tossing down lightning bolts, as Zeus threatened, the God of the Bible takes on our pain, absorbs evil, restores humans, and sets before us another way to live in the world he designed for Eikons. As G. K. Chesterton once said, "The Christian ideal has not been tried and found wanting. It has been found difficult; and left untried." Jesus invites us into the kingdom.

These are broad claims: God is with us, God restores us, and God creates a new community. If these are the claims—

Embracing Grace

and nothing less will do if we want our authentic story to be told—then the question becomes how it all works.

The question of "how it works" is actually another question, one not quite so mechanical. The Bible's answer to how the gospel works is to tell a story—but because there are lots of writers involved who have lots of experiences to describe, there are lots of stories. The so-called "theories of the Atonement" are actually "stories of the Atonement." Let's look now at some of these stories in order to comprehend "how the gospel works."

WHO TELLS THE BEST STORY?

One more time: the claim of the gospel is big, big, big.

A series of theologians have read the Bible and done their best to reduce this bigness down to a single story. But, that story is too grand to be reduced to a single story. In fact, the various stories are each needed, not only because each tells part of the story but also because each tells our story. They are stories of the one gospel. One can't describe grace in one word, and one can't describe the gospel in one word, and one surely can't reduce the work of God for us to one story. It takes a series of stories because the Atonement is more mystery than it is mechanics.

The early Church very quickly began to debate its understanding of God, and the whole Church, everywhere, came to the conclusion that God was a Trinity—Father, Son, Holy Spirit. This is what we read in the Nicene Creed. These creeds were discussed and debated and improved for more than four centuries. This may come as a surprise, but the Church never sensed a need to articulate a single explanatory theory for the Atonement. Some ask why the Church never "solved" the Atonement question. I believe it was because they knew it took more than one story to tell that story, and I believe also that they knew it as a reality so rich in diversity that attempts to narrow it down to manageable size were unwise.

The Church, however, has always taught that God does restore Eikons to union with God and communion with others for the good of others and the world, and that God's work is to form a missional community. "Atonement" means "at-one-ment" with God (and others). Perhaps Irenaeus was the first person to think seriously about what the Bible says about Atonement.

IRENAEUS:
THE STORY OF RECAPITULATION

Irenaeus was born in Asia Minor, a student of the much-revered early Christian martyr Polycarp, who himself was a student of the apostle John. In AD 177 Irenaeus became the bishop of the most important church in Lyons, in Roman Gaul (now France).

The explanation of Irenaeus goes like this: humans were made in God's "image and likeness." The body and soul made up the "image," and the Spirit's gift to us was the "likeness." When Adam and Eve fell, the Spirit departed from them so all that remained was the image. The human condition was incomplete until the coming of Jesus Christ, who was the true image *and* likeness of God—body, soul, and spirit. Most important, because Jesus was the true image and likeness he was given the chance to "recapitulate" the life of Adam and to do so perfectly.

Building on the wonderful theology of the apostle Paul in chapter five of Romans, where Jesus is seen as the Second Adam, Irenaeus understood the Atonement as the story of Jesus' recapitulating Adam's entire life for our benefit. By recapitulating human life, Jesus could establish a new line of humans. Just as Adam and Eve established a line of cracked Eikons so Jesus established a line of restored Eikons.

Irenaeus put it all together in a formula that is impossible to improve: "our Lord Jesus Christ, who did, through his transcendent love, become what we are, that he might bring us to be even what he is himself." In this brief formula, that Jesus became what we are so that we might become what he is, we find everything the Church believed and will believe as it continues to explore the Atonement. The story of recapitulation tells us that "God has been here before."

Imagine with me an adventure through a vast country of still lakes and gentle mountains and dense forests and grassy prairies. Imagine that we are asked to travel through that country to the far side. Imagine also that, since this country is like a labyrinth, there is only one way around those lakes and between those mountains and through those forests and over those prairies. We are given time and freedom, and because there is plenty to explore there is also plenty of time for adventure. As we wend our way through the country, we notice here and there, just beyond a tree or along the lake a footprint or two, at times evidence of a night camp with a burnt log, or some grass where someone slept and that is still pressed down in the shape of a body. We realize, because of these evidences, that however hard we need to concentrate to find our way through that country, we are on the right path because someone has gone before us.

That someone, in the theory of Irenaeus, is Jesus Christ. He has paved the way, carved the path, and charted the course. He has, in other words, recapitulated the life of Adam, perfected the life, and given to us a path to follow. We know this story—the story of finding our way because we find markers on the way—that God "has been here" before. Without those markers we would be lost; with those markers we learn that someone has walked our path before us and lived our life for us.

This is not the only story, and it doesn't tell us everything, but it is one way of probing into the mystery of the Atonement. In fact, it encompasses the others.

EARLY THEOLOGIANS: THE STORY OF RANSOM

The story of ransom, usually called the "classical" theory, can't be pinned to one particular theologian but was especially popular in the first millennium of the Church. This theory is rooted in the grandest story of the Old Testament: Passover and the Exodus, when God liberated Israel from bondage. The ransom story describes a new Exodus in Jesus.

From the time of Adam and Eve on, humans were enslaved spiritually to Satan and demons. To liberate them, God sent his Son, but to do so he had to trick the devil. Spying his chance, Satan snatched the Son and put him to death. But, when Satan grasped the Son, the rest of humanity escaped. As if to insult Satan, Jesus rose from the dead and broke Satan's grip. Victoriously, he returned to the Father. To be fair, most today who adhere to the ransom theory no longer see God's tricking of Satan as part of the mix. Instead, they speak of God's power's being unleashed to liberate humans from sin and suffering and systemic evil. But, one will admit that the story of the early fathers was full of drama. Release from someone's grip is an ageless story.

When my daughter, Laura, was in college, she got the reasonable idea that she wanted to take self-defense lessons. One day she came home and proudly proclaimed that I could grab her wrists as tightly as I wanted, and that no matter how hard I grabbed she could break my grip. Her claim wounded my pride, but I disguised it. First, she said, I'll grab you and see if you can get loose from my grip. She quickly grabbed my wrists, and I struggled but with some male muscle management was able to break free. Then, with a little twinkle of pride in her eyes, she suggested I grip her wrists. I was quite confident I could maintain my grip on her considerably longer than she did on me, but no, before I could say "ransom theory," she got loose. She then explained that most people, when gripped at the wrist, try to wriggle themselves free by turning their arms outwards. But, she explained to me, if you turn toward the person's thumbs you can always break free. (Go ahead, try it. It works.)

And here's the point: according to the story of the ransom, Jesus was the first to break free from the clutching grip of Satan because he knew the only defense mechanism there was: the resurrection. This story of the ransom tells us something important: God's work in Jesus' death and resurrection sets us free from sin and from systemic evil so we can be restored Eikons.

But there are other stories that tell of restoring cracked Eikons.

Embracing Grace

ANSELM:
THE STORY OF SATISFACTION

The single most influential study on the Atonement came from the Archbishop of Canterbury Anselm, who while in exile in about AD 1000, wrote a famous book, *Why God Became Human.* The book explores two philosophical problems: why did God become human? how can an all-holy God reconcile himself with sinful humans? For anyone who takes Genesis 3 and God's utter holiness seriously, Anselm's story of satisfaction has something to say about the problem God was resolving in the Atonement.

In essence, here is Anselm's theory: God's *honor was wounded* by Adam and Eve's sin. They were made to be Eikons but dishonored God through sin. Either God must punish them to balance the scales of justice, or God's honor needs to be restored in another way. For God's honor to be restored, humans must offer to God a genuine satisfaction (or compensation) for what they have done. But, and here the path becomes very steep, because humans are finite, they can't make satisfaction to a God whose infinite honor has been wounded. The God-Man, Jesus Christ, is the perfect substitute: he is both finite—human, and infinite—divine. He alone can restore the honor of God, and he does so by becoming "like us so he can make us like God."

Some theologians have fought Anselm's central insight, blaming him for turning the Cross into a legal courtroom in which God has to work out his (rather psychological) problems in front of the whole world. But the question Anselm raises— How can a holy God forgive sinful humans with utter integrity?—will not go away easily. After all, Paul said something very much like this in the third chapter of Romans when he expressed the logical difficulty in God's forgiving humans: the Cross was, Paul said, "to prove at the present time that he [God] himself is righteous and that he justifies the one who has faith in Jesus." That is, the Cross shows that God can *both* be righteous (God is just) *and* make others righteous (God justifies).

Anselm's theory tells the story of one problem (God's honor) and how that honor can be restored (through the sacrifice of the God-Man). If we take our sin and God's holiness seriously, we can see what drew Anselm into this story. Along with recapitulation and ransom, satisfaction also tells our story. Because the satisfaction theory and the substitution theory have been wound together by theologians, we will illustrate both of these with one story.

THE EVANGELICAL REFORMERS: THE STORY OF PENAL SUBSTITUTION

In every story of the Atonement, Jesus is somehow a *substitute,* or our *representative:* he does for us what we cannot do for ourselves so that we can become what he is. However important substitution is to theology in some circles today, the idea rarely comes to the surface in Irenaeus, in the ransom theory, or in Anselm. But with the German reformer Martin Luther, who preferred the bold and confrontational, and the Swiss reformer John Calvin, who analyzed doctrines with razor-like sharpness, substitutionary Atonement becomes central. Because humans have sinned and wounded God's honor by breaking God's law, they contend, they deserve God's wrath—which is the new emphasis given by the Reformers. As our substitute, Jesus absorbed the wrath of God's punishment against sin, restored God's honor, and so enabled us to escape God's wrath.

To emphasize that the work is more than deflection of wrath, the Reformers emphasized that God also imputed to humans the perfection of Christ so they would be worthy of God's presence. They are, in other words, justified by faith in Christ. This is the story of substitution. It is the story of deflecting wrath for our benefit so that we can enjoy the presence of God.

When I was a youngster, my parents took my two sisters and me to Cape Kennedy (now Cape Canaveral). I remember seeing the launching pad of rockets like that of John Glenn, Mercury-Atlas 6, and Friendship 7, and imagining how they worked. A rocket, standing vertically and aimed into the sky over Florida, would ignite its mighty engines, and powerful heat forces would explode violently downward from its fuel tanks. The launching pad, constructed of dense metal, was shaped like a small pyramid so that it could divert the flames outward, protect the rocket from the flames, and keep the ground from becoming an incinerated dump. We've all seen it on TV: there is a massive explosion and diversion of flames and heat.

Similarly for the story of penal substitution, the cross of Jesus Christ is a "heat-deflecting" instrument: God pours out his wrath on sinners at the cross, but Jesus Christ, the God-Man, deflects that wrath from all humans who will but stand under the cross. For some, this story of penal substitution offends their sensibilities: it depicts an angry God who vents his wrath on his Son. In spite of the regular claim of theologians who contend that the deflection of wrath is all prompted by the love and grace of God and is not a temper tantrum by a vindictive God, many simply are unwilling to listen to this theory. But I think we can agree on this: that Jesus dies for us is clear; that his death is somehow a substitute for us is also clear. Whether or not we agree with penal substitution or not, the theory teaches that Jesus deflects the wrath of God. What we can agree on is that this theory does not tell the whole story of the gospel.

If the recapitulation theory encompasses all elements of the story, there is one more part of that story that needs to be told.

ABELARD:
THE STORY OF THE EXAMPLE

Abelard, a twelfth-century philosopher and theologian, is better known today for his scandalous love affair with the Canon of Notre Dame's daughter, Heloise, than he is for his theology. But, amidst the tohu va-bohu of his life, Abelard proposed a story of the Atonement that still finds admirers today. In essence, it is this: Jesus died as an example, and by contemplating his example we can learn to love God and others, and even sacrifice our lives for the good of others. Hymns such as "When I Survey the Wondrous Cross," or the discipleship teaching of the New Testament that emphasizes following the Jesus of the Cross, or Peter's overt statement in chapter two of his first letter that Jesus is an example all confirm that the Cross is an example.

We all need examples to learn.

My son, who when I wrote *The Jesus Creed* was still playing minor league baseball for the Chicago Cubs, is now an Area Scout for the Cubs. His responsibility is to watch amateurs and file reports to the organization on a player's prospects of making it to the big leagues. This spring he was home one evening and explained to me that one of the players he was scouting had "too long a swing." For baseball people, this is in-house language that a given player won't make it unless he can change his swing. When I asked him what a "long swing" was, he explained it but it didn't make much sense to me. To explain a baseball swing by talking about trunk rotation and hand placement and hand motion and their relationship to where the ball must be hit in relationship to the plate doesn't work for me. So, I said, "Show me." Which he did—and now I'll try to explain it briefly. A batter's swing is "short" if his hands descend in a straight line toward the ball. His swing is "long" if his hands go down a bit and then up toward the ball. Micro-seconds, to be sure, but when a ball is coming at you at over ninety miles per hour, the shorter the better. My point is simple: I didn't understand what a "short" swing was until I saw Lukas demonstrate it.

The Cross is a vivid (to put it mildly) demonstration of a life of sacrifice. For some, this is the major point of the Cross: it exemplifies sacrifice and courage and sticking to one's principles and confidence in God's ultimate triumph. The at-one-ment is more than this, but the death of Jesus is at least *exemplary.*

Each of these stories—recapitulation, ransom, satisfaction, substitution, and example—does what it can to tell God's story of the at-one-ment, the story of God's drawing us into union with God and communion with others for the good of others and the world.

THE STORY WHO IS A PERSON

Sometimes theologians, and you may have already said this about what you have read here, speak as if the Atonement is abstract theory. The story of the gospel is first and foremost and nothing if it is not first the *embracing of persons.* God embraces us in Jesus Christ and we embrace God in Jesus Christ. The embrace involves trust and love and commitment. God is personal; Eikons are persons; Jesus is a person. Restoring Eikons is about restoring persons so they are in union and communion. At-one-ment is a "re-unioning" and "re-communioning" of our relationships. God does all this in the context of a community and with a missional direction: so "atoned" persons can be of good to others and the world. Any theory that stops short of these other elements of the gospel fails to explain what the Atonement is all about.

A big gospel takes many stories to explain.

To be sure, the gospel manages sin, declares humans right, and liberates. But more than these, the gospel is the embracing of persons: of God and humans, of humans with other humans, for the good of others and the world.

THE SILENCE OF THE CREEDS
AS A CLUE

The early Christian thinkers who articulated the faith believed by all, everywhere, and always, chose not to articulate a "theory of the Atonement." And for good reason. The New Testament theologians raided their own vocabularies to explain how the Atonement worked. And one story was not enough. There is wisdom in letting a variety of stories roam throughout our faith to explain what took place for us and to us in the season of grace.

Who says this better than the American theologian Kevin Vanhoozer? He says, "We gather around the Lord's Table as we have been instructed . . . , awaiting the elements that signify more than our starving theories. Then, like the five thousand, we discover that after our centuries-long banquet of Atonement theology, there are still more fragments of the cross left over." "Let us," he asks us, "fill our baskets and keep the feast."

"I am," Jesus said, "the bread of life."

9

THE DIVINE GOSPEL COMEDY

WE ALL GO THROUGH SEASONS—approximately ten years of childhood and then another ten years (if we are lucky) of adolescence, and then we enter into all kinds of seasons: early adulthood, middle adulthood, and senior citizenship. Some of our seasons descend into gloom and others soar into glory.

The gospel story itself journeys through its own seasons of gloom and glory.

The point deserves to be emphasized: it takes God seasons to create gospel conditions. If we neglect any of the gospel seasons, the gospel gets distorted and its purpose and direction lose focus. There are three seasons in the gospel: the Cross, the Resurrection, and Pentecost. These three seasons are surrounded by other seasons: Creation, the Fall, and the history of Israel and the Church. But, if it is important to say that the Christian faith is cruci-form (cross shaped), it is just as important to say that God's work involved the Cross, the Resurrection, and the gift of the Holy Spirit.

Notice what Paul says in Romans, chapter four, in a verse that is the leading theme of *Embracing Grace:* "[Jesus Christ] was handed over to death for our trespasses and was raised for our justification." Notice that Paul knows something happened on Good Friday and something else happened on Easter morning, and that the two belong together. The story of the gospel includes and needs both, and it is not the gospel without both. What Paul doesn't say here, but he will say it in other contexts, is that Pentecost belongs with the Cross and Easter morning.

THE GOSPEL ONE MORE TIME

Reflecting on the Cross and Resurrection and Pentecost (to come), we are led to this definition of the gospel of embracing grace: the gospel is the work of the triune, interpersonal God to form a community in which cracked Eikons,*s* are restored *through the Cross and Resurrection and Pentecost* to union with God and communion with others for the good of the world.

THE GOSPEL STORY:
TRAGEDY OR COMEDY?

The ancient Greeks wrote plays in two forms—tragedies and comedies. Simply speaking, and hiding all the nuance, ridicule, and social context, a *tragedy* tells a story with a bad ending, and a *comedy* tells a story with a good ending. Thus, when some say that Homer's *The Odyssey* is a "comedy" they do not mean that is humorous or funny, but that Odysseus escapes death and returns home and makes things right (even though it takes buckets of blood to do this). Stories with good endings are comedies.

The Christian Gospels, because of the Resurrection, can be classified as "comedies." They aren't funny in any sense of the word, but what looks like a tragedy when Jesus dies suddenly morphs into a comedy because of the Resurrection. One thinks here of Dante's *The Divine Comedy*, which offers hope to those who can journey with Dante and Beatrice to the heavenly realms. Or, the 2004 baseball season of the Boston Red Sox which became a comedy—as well as a time for celebration—because they won the World Series, and the same season for the Chicago Cubs, which became a tragedy because. . . . well, all their seasons seem to be tragedies! Or, C. S. Lewis's *The Chronicles of Narnia,* which is a comedy, because both the individual books and the entire set open up a vista on a world in which hope and justice and love will eventually be established. These are all (except for the part about the Cubs) "comedies" in the classical sense.

One can easily contrast "comedy" with Ernest Hemingway's real-world but gloomy "tragedy," *The Old Man and the Sea,* in which the old man Santiago, who had gone eighty-four days without landing anything, catches the fish of his life, an uncontrollably large marlin. In the process of struggling with this giant marlin, Santiago is wounded by the fishing line as it tears into his skin, and so he begins to identify with the marlin, a marlin that he himself eventually kills with a harpoon and lashes to the side of his boat. He begins his journey home, only to have the bloody trail of the marlin attract sharks with which Santiago must struggle. By nighttime, Santiago has lost; the sharks devour the marlin, the greatest accomplishment of the old man's life. All that remains of his catch is the skeleton, which the locals tragically identify as that of a shark. Death, Hemingway is saying, is inevitable, and all we can do is struggle against it. Humans can become heroic in their battle against the odds, but no one comes out on top. Some may read Hemingway's novella differently than I, but no one considers it a comedy.

Some might find intense delight in the tragic dimension of life, wrestling like Captain Ahab in *Moby Dick* the uncooperative whale of the world in which we live, or in relishing the tragedies found in the tohu va-bohu of the cracked Eikon but the gospel makes the claim that life is ultimately a "comedy," a comedy of grace. It is the Divine Gospel Comedy. The last word in the gospel comedy is not death, but life. The last word is not the Cross, but the Resurrection, because Good Friday finds its "comedic" answer in Easter morning and Pentecost.

THE DEATH AND
THE RESURRECTION

Humans have a problem, and the problem is inherent to who we are. The solution is not just to say "we had a good start" or "we are a mess" or "we can be forgiven" or "we can be liberated" or "we can experience the divine." No, the solution is to restore humans in the context of a community so they can journey into union with God. God does his gospel work over an entire season: Good Friday, which explores and forgives the cracks in the Eikon; Easter morning, which renews and empowers us to walk again; and Pentecost, which empowers us to be a kingdom community. It takes more than Good Friday for this gospel work. The French theologian Francis Xavier Durrwell said this perfectly: "A person dead to God cannot come to life again merely because someone else has died in his or her place." What a dead person needs is new life. That is what the gospel promises.

The text quoted immediately above from the apostle Paul is not a solo statement. He says this often. Because the Corinthian Christians were confused about the Resurrection, Paul devoted a lengthy chapter (15) in 1 Corinthians to the resurrection. In verse 14, Paul says that "if Christ has not been raised, then our [Paul's] proclamation has been in vain and your [the Corinthians'] faith has been in vain." And in verse 17 he goes one step further: "If Christ has not been raised, your faith is futile and you are still in your sins." So connected are the Death and the Resurrection for Paul, that Paul says the Cross needs the Resurrection for the forgiveness of sins!

If the Cross deals with the cracks in the Eikon the Resurrection makes them glow with new life and hope. When the Resurrection meets the Cross we see the profoundest comedy ever written.

RESURRECTION AS GOSPEL COMEDY OVERCOMING TRAGEDY

In 1964, the U.S.A. came to a stop as it watched a dramatic scene unravel in the Congo. Paul Carlson, an American medical missionary, was serving thousands of the Congolese in Wasolo, a village not far south of the Mbomu and Ubangi Rivers that separated the Congo from the Central African Republic. Paul, along with his wife, Lois, and their children, had been in the Congo for a few years when some rebels began to take action. Paul and Lois were separated by the political troubles: Lois and the children were in the Central African Republic in September when Paul decided to return to the hospital to care for his patients.

On September 18, Paul and others were captured by the rebels, and the twisting tale of what happened and when and why began. Somehow, the rebels labeled Paul a military major, a mercenary, and he was accused of espionage. He was taken to Stanleyville, the center of the rebellion. In a letter not seen until later, Paul wrote to Lois: "Forgive me for the worry I have caused. I was wrong to try to stay, but I feel I put it all into God's hands and must leave it there. . . . I've had beatings and known what it means not to know the future for tomorrow. . . . If by God's grace I live, which I doubt, it will be to His glory. . . . God guide each and pray with me that each day we live for Him we might be a witness." Paul was "tried," unjustly found "guilty," and was to face execution.

In the cruel savagery of the rebels, Paul and the others were taken on November 18 to a mock execution, only to be taken back to their place of confinement. Paul and his companions were able to spend time together praying and worshiping and exhorting one another with words from Paul Carlson's New Testament. The Simba rebel guards soon came into their room to lead them outside into the street. With planes hovering overhead poised for a rescue, the rebel Colonel Opepe was somehow shot, panic broke out, and guns were firing. Some of the hostages were shot, but Paul and others managed to escape.

They ran for the nearest protection. A small group ran to the shelter of a house and clambered over the porch wall.

Chuck Davis was by that narrow wall, where there was room for only one at a time to vault over. Paul came running alongside, saying, "Go." Chuck leaped the wall, reached back, had his fingers on Paul's sweater when a young Simba, coming around the corner with a gun, fired five shots.

Paul's work on earth was finished. . . .

[Chuck] later said that when he saw Paul lying there, "I fell down and cried like a baby."

Gene saw Paul fall. As the rounds of shooting subsided . . . [he] saw Paul's Testament in his pocket, and gently removed it, for he knew Paul's wish that it be returned to [Lois].

Paul Carlson's powerful testimony, told in *Time* on December 4, 1964, on which cover he appeared, was sustained by his confidence in the Resurrection of Jesus Christ and the hope it grants.

The work of Paul Carlson continues to this day. There are nearly 200,000 Christians in Covenant churches in the

Congo; the health care system, with four hospitals, is one of the finest in the area; nearly 50,000 kids are attending schools founded by the missionaries; there are nearly one million people being served by eleven Congolese doctors and 173 nurses. All because of resurrection faith.

PETER AND HEBREWS, TOO

The apostle Peter also connects death and resurrection at the beginning of his first letter: "To the exiles . . . who have been chosen and destined by God the Father and sanctified by the Spirit to be obedient to Jesus Christ and to be sprinkled with his blood: . . . Blessed be the God and Father of our Lord Jesus Christ! By his great mercy he has given us a new birth into a living hope through the resurrection of Jesus Christ from the dead."

The "new birth," what I am describing as the restoring work of the gospel, Peter is saying, takes place because of the power of the Resurrection of Jesus Christ, whose blood (death) was sprinkled on believers. Death *and* resurrection. You might recall that Peter's first few encounters with the Cross, or with Jesus' prediction of that Cross and the event itself, were not happy events. One time he told Jesus that death was not an option for Messiahs, and later he announced in front of everyone that he had no connection whatsoever with Jesus—and this when Jesus was standing trial. Only *after the Resurrection* did Peter embrace the Cross. So, when Peter tells us that our new birth occurs through the Resurrection, he is probably giving us a firsthand testimony of the impact of the Resurrection on his own faith.

Another New Testament writer, the author of Hebrews, in chapter five makes the same connection between the death of Jesus and the Resurrection: "Although he [Jesus] was a Son, he learned obedience through what he suffered; and having been made perfect, he became the source of eternal salvation for all who obey him." Jesus suffered all the way to death, but through this suffering he learned obedience; his obedience permitted him to be "made perfect" through his resurrection.

Let's tie this all together by referring once more to the apostle Paul, and especially to the sixth chapter of Romans. Here Paul claims the following: we were baptized into both Jesus' death and his resurrection, and this unites each one of us to his death and his life. Our "old self" was crucified on the cross when Jesus died—our own tragedy—so that our "body of death" could be destroyed and we could be set free from sin—our own comedy. Because Jesus both died and was raised, Paul tells the Christians, "you also must consider yourselves dead to sin and alive to God in Christ Jesus."

There we have it all: the restoration of cracked Eikons is empowered by the twin events of the Death and the Resurrection.

So, it would be more appropriate for Christians to say that Jesus came not just to die for our sins, but to die for our sins and to be raised to empower us to live as Eikons,s. The gospel is God's comedy, because in the gospel death is overcome by life, and that life restores us to community for the good of the world.

In the history of Christian art, the most enduring Christian symbol is the cross, sometimes taking the form of a crucifix (emphasizing the suffering of Jesus Christ) and other times taking the form of an empty cross (emphasizing his victory over death). We need both, and what we also need is another form of Christian art today, a cross with the symbol of fire above it—telling us that Jesus' death and resurrection, along with the gift of the Spirit, is what creates the cycle of grace.

10

A FIVE-FOOT
GOSPEL

WE HAVE DISCOVERED THAT THE GOSPEL IS THE *WORK* OF GOD. But the apostle Paul, in the opening section of Romans, claims even more than that: he says the gospel is "the power of God for salvation to everyone who has faith." It is the power of God to create a new situation, the kingdom of God.

Paul was empowered to make sure everyone understood that God's powerful work is for *everyone,* and the problem he faced was including Gentiles in the people of God. While in prison in Rome for preaching a gospel that included Gentiles, Paul told the Ephesians, in chapter six of his letter to them, that he was preaching the "gospel of peace" in the face of systemic evil. In the fourteenth chapter of Revelation, we find an angel proclaiming the gospel "to *every* nation and tribe and language and people."

The gospel is, as I have said before, *for all of us,* and it is designed to create a community for each of us. The problem is that cracked Eikons prefer others with similar cracks, and this creates ethnic divisions within society instead of a community for our society.

That community is the product of the Spirit who unites us. "To each," Paul says in the twelfth chapter of his first letter to the Corinthians, "is given the manifestation of the Spirit for the common good." "For in the one Spirit we were all baptized into one body—Jews or Greeks, slaves or free—and we were all made to drink of one Spirit." This one body knows no hierarchy in ethnicity, gender, or economic status, as Paul declares in his kingdom manifesto in the third chapter of Galatians: "There is no longer Jew or Greek, there is no longer slave or free, there is no longer male and female; for all of you are one in Christ Jesus."

We know that Jesus himself performed a gospel for the common good, and we know the Spirit is sent to create a community for the common good.

Jesus, in the Gospel of John, chapter fourteen, tells his disciples that he will be raised and will return to his Father, and that he will send them the "Advocate" (or "Paraclete"), the Holy Spirit. Christian existence is about Spirit-existence: "This [One Jesus will send] is the Spirit of truth . . . You know him, because he abides with you, and he will be in you. I will not leave you orphaned; I am coming to you. . . . On that day you will know that I am in my Father, and you in me, and I in you."

Many points can be made but these are surely the most important: the Paraclete is Jesus' presence in his followers; the Paraclete unites the followers of Jesus with Father, Son, and Holy Spirit; this union with God creates the possibility for his followers to love God and one another. In other words, Jesus' resurrection empowers the sending of the Paraclete, who leads us to union with God and communion with one another—and the "world" will see this and take notice.

This is what the apostle Paul means when he declares that the gospel is the "power" of God. Perhaps one of the notable features of the presence of the Holy Spirit in that first Christian community, as we read in the early chapters of Acts, was a boldness to try new things and go new places (where the Gentiles lived!) with a gospel that set loose a cycle of grace. It was the Holy Spirit who empowered them to draw swords with systemic evil structures—like ethnic, gender, and class injustices. It was the Spirit who empowered them to establish little pockets of the kingdom throughout the entire Roman Empire.

Embracing Grace

That same Spirit was needed then and is needed now if our compass is pointed toward God's kingdom—on earth as it is in heaven.

TRY SAYING "NO!" TO ARAMINTA

Araminta was born around 1820, but no one really knows (other than God) *when* she was really born. We do know when Araminta died: 1913. No one knows *where* she was born either, except that it was in Maryland near Bucktown, and we are not sure which of her brothers and sisters were older and younger. We don't know these things because Araminta's parents were African slaves, and no one kept records for slaves. Slaves also had no clothing other than what they wore, and, because they were ordered to work as soon as they could, they also had no childhood. When Araminta was five, a neighbor appeared and picked her, the way farmers pick fruit from a tree, to care for her child. In caring for this child, Araminta realized that "my hair had nebber been combed an' it stood out like a bushel basket." Araminta cared for other children, and in one of her homes she was whipped almost every day. She had no recourse to justice.

Slaves had no health protection and even worse they had no security: family members could be sold on the auction block at the will of the master. Fear of separation from one's children terrorized slave parents. Araminta saw two of her own sisters carried off, and she never saw or heard from them again. No one knows what happened; no one other than Araminta's family even cared. When a young slave girl got pregnant, owners often thought slave girls were lying and so kept them working without relief for their physical needs. No one seemed to notice.

But, the power of systemic evil can be resisted with the power of the gospel.

When Edward Brodess, master of Araminta's mother Rit (a shortened form of Harriet), made it known that a Georgia man wanted to take her son, Rit defied his power by hiding her son in the woods. When Brodess discovered Rit's secret, he came to her cabin, only to meet courage with a name—"Rit": "The first man that comes into my house," she said, "I will split his head open."

Then and there the five-foot-and-no-inches Araminta, who later changed her name to Harriet (as in Tubman), learned an important lesson from her mother: no one was going to say "no" to her when it defied her gospel principles. She absorbed the "faith of her fathers" (and mothers) by listening to Bible stories (as they were told by slave preachers) in clandestine meetings from "sundown to sunup," stories that were inevitably drawn from two major sources: the Exodus led by Moses and the kingdom vision of Jesus. When masters used the Bible to demand subordination, the slaves turned the masters' theology on its head by appealing to the power they found in Moses and Jesus. That power, so they believed and so they discovered, was the power of God for salvation for *everyone*. Such a power also meant freedom from injustice and oppression and a freedom for inclusion and equality.

Araminta, who later changed her name to Harriet, pursued such a freedom with every power she could muster: "I had reasoned this out in my mind; there was one of the things I had a right to, liberty or death; if I could not have one, I would have the other."

Today Harriet Tubman, whose story has been told so well by Catherine Clinton, is known for her work on the "Underground Railroad" and for freeing hundreds of slaves, but her story is fired by the power of the Resurrection and the Spirit of Pentecost. This faith ennobled a short, solitary slave-woman to do the unthinkable: to fight systemic evil, and to carry on in faith until the goal was reached. Her goals were freedom and equality. Here is a woman who looked, listened, learned, and linked to her own local problems, and she had a hand in changing the world.

The Underground Railroad was operated by "abductors" and "conductors," those who extracted slaves and those who guided them to places of freedom. Harriet herself made at least one trip per year into slave territory (she called it

"Egypt"), and many of her trips ended at St. Catherine's in Ontario, Canada (her Canaan), after the escaped slaves had crossed the Niagara (her Jordan). Harriet Tubman absorbed the gospel story so deeply it became her own story.

Perhaps the most remarkable feature of Harriet Tubman's work, other than using opiates to keep the babies quiet or the Combahee River Raid in which 150 black soldiers commandeered by Harriet freed 756 slaves, is that she was famous for leading slaves to freedom without ever getting caught. For her work she received the name "Moses."

It is a pity now to learn that Harriet Tubman's successes, climaxing in the Emancipation Proclamation, did not thrust her into national sponsorship. Instead, the battles began all over with new "no's" she would have to resist: no vote for women, no rest for her wearied body, no pay for her endless efforts, and no funds to carry on the work of helping ex-slaves to become acculturated. But, Harriet Tubman's pentecostal power had "no limits." A woman who helped her in Auburn, New York, where she had settled, said this: "All these years her doors have been open to the needy. . . . The aged . . . the babe deserted, the demented, the epileptic, the blind, the paralyzed, the consumptive all have fond shelter and welcome. At no one time can I recall the little home to have sheltered less than six or eight wrecks of humanity entirely dependent upon Harriet for their all."

Harriet Tubman, whose favorite story of the Atonement was the ransom story, was liberated, and she was a liberator because she wouldn't take "no" for an answer. Her work of liberation, which quickly shifted direction toward suffrage, had power because the gospel she believed in contrasted with the gospel of those around her: slave owners, when they thought about it, had a gospel of hierarchy for the white man, while many of her co-slaves had a gospel that emphasized salvation in the afterlife. Harriet believed that heaven was also a place on earth for those who would pray and work for that kingdom to come on earth as it was in heaven. For her, the gospel was about heart and soul and mind, but also about strength—and that meant setting the whole person free for the good of the world.

THE GRACE OF EMBRACING GRACE

No matter how much we admire Harriet Tubman, or anyone else who has worked hard to create the gospel cycle of grace, that sort of work is empowered by God's Spirit in us. It is hard to maintain the balance between passive hope and passionate activism, but the apostle Paul states this perfectly when he describes his own efforts to work for a unified and loving and holy Church: "For this I toil and struggle with all the energy that he [Christ] powerfully inspires within me."

This is how Paul closed the first chapter of his letter to the Colossians: the gospel is God's *powerful work* in us and for us. We are empowered by God's power, as Harriet Tubman was empowered by God's power.

The Bible describes this often with the word *grace*. Some theologians have overemphasized grace to the effect that humans seem to be lost causes, miserable wretches, and bankrupt blotches living on planet earth until God turns out the lights. It is true that humans are sinners, and we can surely act out the worst imaginable sins. But focusing on human sinfulness goes contrary to the grain of the Bible, which clearly sees humans as Eikons in need of restoration to be sure, but the object of God's special love. The Bible, after all, is a "comedy," not a "tragedy." And the purpose of that grace is not just to fill in the cracks but also to empower us to live a gospel life.

In the Bible, *grace* is who God is and what God wants to do for us. The enemy of grace, once again, is individualism. We cannot erase our sins—the Cross does this; we cannot renew ourselves to life—the Resurrection does this; and we cannot on our own live a loving life of holiness and power or come to terms with the truth of the gospel and wage war against injustice—the Holy Spirit does this. God's doing all of this for us—forgiving our sins, awakening a new life in us, enlightening our minds for a new life, enabling us to live in such a way as to reflect his glory—is grace. Plenty of theologians

Embracing Grace

have tried to define grace, but I especially like the definition of a pastor-friend, Keith Carpenter: grace, Keith says, is the absolute and unrelenting goodness of God toward humans. It is the word "unrelenting" that I like so much.

For many years I had a small bust of a beret-wearing Frenchman I called Pierre hanging in my office. He had a little twinkle in his eye and a bit of mischief in his smile, and no one could look at Pierre without smiling back. Then one day the wind slammed the door shut and Pierre crashed to the floor. I walked over to my office companion, found him in a multitude of pieces, realized that I could not put him back together again, said a brief "Thanks for all the smiles!" and then tossed him into the garbage can with a thud and a clang.

Embracing grace is not like this at all. When Adam and Eve "fell" and the Eikon cracked, God came alongside them with the famous question, "Adam, where are you?" Adam answered back. He and Eve had been found in pieces. But, instead of picking up the pieces and saying "too bad for you!" God embraced these cracked Eikons and unleashed his love and grace to renew Adam and Eve to their former glory (and more).

Harriet Tubman was empowered by such grace. We can be, too.

God's grace is a power designed to restore us for the good of others and the world.

11
DIMINISHED BY EXCLUSION

Adam and Eve were created to be Eikons of God, humans who would reflect God's glory by loving God and one another as they governed God's good world. They chose, however, to walk away from that love of God. The choice diminished their glory, and they were never the same again. They didn't love God as they were designed, and they didn't love one another as they were designed, and the tohu va-bohu began to permeate God's good world. And it continues to permeate the world even in our own day.

Embracing Grace

Some Eikons prefer to live in the cracks.

They do this in different ways. Some hang out with one another to create a juggernaut of injustice or a dark mist of evil. Others prefer to be alone, to be broken, and to sink into meaninglessness or cynicism or anger. Some stubbornly refuse to own up to their own truth no matter how much they hear it might help them. This part of the story is hard to tell, because it is both genuine and sad and tragic.

Some of us prefer the chaotic roar of the tohu va-bohu to the music of grace.

Humans take one of two options in responding to the story of the gospel. The options are, as Miroslav Volf has so ably explained, exclusion or embrace. Either we *exclude* ourselves from God and others, distancing ourselves from Eden and preferring the tohu va-bohu, and diminish our own Eikon or we *embrace* God and others and the cycle of grace, head back toward Eden, and discover in the journey that there is hope for a final banquet.

Some prefer to dine alone. They prefer diminishment.

EXCLUSION

No reality of life is any clearer than this: some people just don't care for God or for others or for the world. For them, it can all fall back into the tohu va-bohu. "To hell with it!" is their attitude. Which is what the tohu va-bohu is.

This sort of person tends to *define* himself or herself as an individualist whose exclusion from God, others, and the world is who they are. Exclusionists find identity in the pattern of exclusion. Instead of seeing themselves as "like God" and "made for one another" and part of a missional community of faith, exclusionists define themselves *over against God and others* to carve out some special sanctuary where they can operate sovereignly. Instead of telling the story of the divine gospel comedy they prefer to tell the tragedy of brokenness and loneliness. However, the place of utter exclusion does not exist, except in the mind driven by a will to find what doesn't exist. God, who is sometimes called the Hound of Heaven, will find each of us to ask, "Where are you?"

But the one who chooses to live out a tragedy diminishes the Eikon.

No one lived this story more vividly than Mary McCarthy, the brilliant American satirist and essayist, who consciously and quite vocally excluded herself from God.

When I left the competitive atmosphere of the parochial school, my religion withered on the stalk. . . . Hence, as a lapsed Catholic, I do not trouble myself about the possibility that God may exist after all. If He exists (which seems to me more than doubtful), I am in for a bad time in the next world. . . . For myself, I prefer not to play it so safe, and I shall never send for a priest or recite an Act of

Contrition in my last moments. I do not mind if I lose my soul for all eternity. If the kind of God exists Who would damn me for not working out a deal with Him, then that is unfortunate. I should not care to spend eternity in the company of such a person.

We may admire such candor, but would you be surprised if I also said she had problematic relations with more than God and her Catholic faith? Ironically, her potent, acrid words betray her ongoing concern to define herself over against God and the Church. She claimed to be an exclusionist.

For my part, I'm not sure how to read words like hers—Eikons, I say to myself, can never really become anything else even when they seek to diminish themselves. I've read her memoirs and a biography about this most capable of writers, and I find her a tragedy. At the time Mary McCarthy was one of America's leading critics, other writers with identical backgrounds, like Flannery O'Connor and Walker Percy and Thomas Merton and Dorothy Day, who in their own way embraced the gospel, charted an entirely different path for themselves. Paul Elie has told their story so beautifully in *The Life You Save May Be Your Own*. I read their stories and I say, "Why Mary McCarthy?"

My experience of the Mary McCarthys is this: we need to be cautious. Many of those who appear to exclude themselves from God are hiding the wounds of earlier embraces. It is harder than we think to deny what God made us to be. But sometimes there is, as C. S. Lewis calls it, a *Great Divorce.*

In exclusion's most radical form, humans can exclude themselves from God and others so categorically that they can gain a sense—again only a sense—that God no longer exists. We call this "atheism." But, humans can't really be atheists. Instead, they become individualists; their absorption with an All-consuming Self drowns out their Eikonic sense of God, and, before long, they begin to tell themselves that there is no God and that they are atheists. What they really are is individualists.

Radical exclusion, however, is rare. Most of us, if we become authentic truth-tellers, are a mixture of both exclusion and embrace. The more we exclude ourselves, the more we diminish ourselves and make ourselves incapable of God's presence or the presence of others.

SIGNS OF EXCLUSION

How do we as humans exclude God and others? We "exclude" God when we refuse to embrace God or when, like Adam and Eve, we run and hide. We exclude others by subjugating them under our own verbal and physical power. Humans also exclude by assimilating others into their own ego, sometimes so powerfully that humans join Cain by murdering the other. In other words, exclusion is isolation, expulsion,

Embracing Grace

idolatry, libel, slavery, domination, emotional blackmail, closed-door dealing, propaganda, intentionally false information, refusal to listen to the other side, and murder. Sometimes exclusion is so subtle it can only be described as Miroslav Volf defines it, as an "all-pervasive low-intensity evil." Exclusion, in other words, ranges from petty sins to systemic evil, from telling a fib to betraying your country, from individuals' refusing to give a small portion for the poor to dictators' converting food for the poor into palaces for the privileged few.

Exclusion can be subtle.

Because Jesus knew that union with God and communion with others was the essence of our existence, he spoke (in Matthew chapter five) of anger as "murder":

> You have heard that it was said to those of ancient times, "You shall not murder"; and "whoever murders shall be liable to judgment." But I say to you that if you are angry with a brother or sister, you will be liable to judgment; and if you insult a brother or sister, you will be liable to the council; and if you say, "You fool," you will be liable to the hell of fire.

Anger, too, is a form of exclusion because by it we say things and do things that prevent communion with others. Jesus finds the produce of exclusion in lust, in divorce, in not telling the truth, in vindictiveness, and in justifying hate for one set of humans by justifying love for another set. Volf gets it right when he speaks of an "all-pervasive low-intensity evil."

There are other signs of exclusion besides these given by Jesus. Husbands and wives exclude one another when their trivial spat turns stone cold and the evening seeps away in silence and one evening of silence lingers into days and weeks or months. Parents and children exclude one another when their struggles for sympathy become titanic wars of accusation where all sense of proportion is lost. Political parties exclude one another and the citizens listening to them when they refuse to listen to one another, when they avoid nuance in stating differences, and when they resort to inflammatory slogans. Warring countries exclude one another when they enslave, when they imprison protesting voices, and when they take up arms with one another. Instead of opening the heart to a wideness that permits the other to enter in safely, instead of the embrace that permits the Eikon to bloom into glory, humans sometimes exclude themselves from one another and so break the chance of being restored to one another.

Others make themselves into someone else. We call this "hypocrisy." The hypocrite is the quintessential actor whose acting diminishes who she or he is. Dangerously so. Why? Because the hypocrite tries to be someone he or she is not, and by so acting out another character, the hypocrite hides

Embracing Grace

himself or herself from self and from others (but not from God). The hypocrite foists upon the world a story of himself or herself that is not true, both hiding the real self and diminishing that same self. Hypocrites fake an outer self and offer that fake self to others and, in so doing, exclude themselves from the God whose will it is to create union with God and communion with others for the good of the world.

Exclusion may be subtle sometimes, but its results penetrate to the depths of the created order as well as the inner chambers of the individual's heart.

EXCLUSION
BY ANOTHER NAME IS . . .

Exclusion needs to be seen for what it really is. Ultimately, exclusion is a paradox. Exclusion in its very essence is the choice to embrace ourselves as the only embrace needed. By turning inward instead of outward—toward God and others, the self-embracing "I" seeks to restore what was lost in Eden by searching for it within oneself. Humans cannot be satisfied with a self-embrace; humans are made for God and others and the good of the world. Restlessness finds its resolution only in rest: "Our heart," said Augustine, "is restless till it finds its rest in you."

Craig Barnes, formerly pastor of National Presbyterian Church in Washington, D.C., tells the tragedy of his father who "spent the first part of his life trying to be at home in the respectable places. Not only was he the head of our home, but he was also the head of our home church, serving as pastor. But failing at all of that, he left when I was a teenager. For almost thirty years I never knew where he was as he abandoned all who loved him. . . . He died alone on Thanksgiving, 2000. . . . If it were up to him, and for the first time it wasn't, he wouldn't have shown up for his funeral. But there he was. So dead, and yet finally so present. It was one last pathetic irony in the life of a father known mostly through absence."

What we perceive as exclusion, as for instance in the above story about Mary McCarthy or in this story about Craig's father, sometimes masks a deeply wounded person who is still yearning to find a way to love God and others. Sometimes exclusion is covering up a guarded embrace.

When Craig and his brother were given the chance to take anything they might want of their father's, such as could be found in the small trailer in which he was living, Craig said no but his brother said yes. To his astonishment, all that remained from his father's life as a pastor was his three-ring, leather notebook full of sermon notes—and ongoing reflections and confessions from his life after he had abandoned the only loves of his life. On the last page was his father's Daily Prayer List, and the top two on the list were Craig and his brother.

Embracing Grace

His father had diminished into a wraith of who he had been. However distant he was from Craig and his brother and his calling, "the memory," Craig states, "of the Father's house was still with him."

Craig's father could not forgive himself for what he had done. Because he couldn't live with the shame, he excluded himself from an entire life of loving his family. Even if there is a wounded embrace under all the layers of a human soul, it still remains a fact that isolation from those we are called to love diminishes both person and home. "We are lost," Craig observes from his experience, and "nothing is harder than finding home again."

This story of Craig's father opens up the essence of what sin really is. Theologians have always tried to find the essence of sin or to find the most significant sin. Most textbooks dealing with this issue narrow it down to pride. My contention is that pride is the proud term we place on what gives pride its true meaning: exclusion. The ultimate sin is to exclude ourselves from God, from others, and from the world. Exclusion is the one term that best describes those who turn inward for redemption but who cannot, no matter how hard they work at it, find what they are looking for. What we are all looking for is God. We are made to.

As Craig Barnes puts it, "That's because we're yearning for home, and home has nothing to do with how good the place is. It has everything to do with whether or not it is the right place. And the right place isn't something you choose, but a place that chooses you, molds you, and tells you who you are." That place is the gospel of embracing grace.

Some choose not to dwell in that place but seek for their own place.

WHAT HAPPENS TO A LIFE OF EXCLUSION?

It wounds even to find another example of exclusion, but abound. Tony Hendra, who seems to be climbing out of a life of exclusion, tells his story in the revealing book *Father Joe*. As a fourteen-year-old, Tony was caught *en flagrant* with a friend's wife. Instead of beating Tony to a pulp, the man led Tony to Father Joe (Dom Joseph Warrilow) at Quarr Abbey, a Benedictine monastery on the Isle of Wight. Under the care of Father Joe, Tony began to make progress in the spiritual life, but (in the wisdom of Father Joe) was not approved for the monastic life, and so Tony headed off to Cambridge University.

This fork in the road took Tony down a long, painful, solitary path of infidelity, drugs, and all manner of soul soothers that neither soothe nor care for the soul. The main tune he played on that road was satire, a blend of comedy and tragedy with an emphasis on the latter. Satire is a form of literature and communication dominated by humor, irony, and ridicule. Tony eventually became a lead writer for *National Lampoon*, precursor of U.S.A.'s Saturday Night Live. But if life is spent finding the foibles of others, if when foibles are found a person learns to feast on such meals, then soon our entire bodies are filled with poison and venom directed at others. Satire cannot be innocent because humans are Eikons, and to ridicule the created is to ridicule the Creator.

The apostle John, in the second chapter of his first letter, uses a graphically simple dichotomy to make this very same point. Notice these words: "But whoever hates another is in the darkness, walks in that darkness, and cannot find the way—because the darkness has brought on blindness." This translation of mine highlights what happens when we walk away from loving God and loving others, when we turn in on ourselves: we are enveloped by a darkness that blinds us to a way out.

The tragedy is that some humans prefer to be diminished.

The hope for every tragedy is the divine gospel comedy.

12

ENLIVENED
BY EMBRACE

Tony Hendra's story in *Father Joe* that we explored briefly at the end of the last chapter not only illustrates the theme of exclusion but also demonstrates that out of such pain can emerge an *embrace*. Father Joe had written letters to Tony about his marriage: "Be unselfish with her, Tony dear. . . . I know you will be unselfish with her and your beautiful little girls." But Tony knew the truth: "No one could have been more selfish—treating his family like props, possessions, inconveniences, mostly forgetting them completely in his precious mission to save the world through laughter." He came to the bottom layer of what he had done with all his relationships. "I had failed. I had failed my vocation. I had failed my family. I had failed, period. I had nothing of worth. No hope, no faith, no God, no intellectual resources, no desire to use them if I had. It was all gone forever, as irretrievable as the wind. I fingered the bottle of Valium."

After struggling his way back to Quarr Abbey, where he had first met Father Joe, Tony pleaded to enter the monastery, but Father Joe said no.

"You're a husband and a father, Tony. . . . A husband and a father is what God has always wanted you to be. It's a vocation as sacred as ours."

"I've failed utterly at both those things, Father Joe. Not once. Twice."

"Yes, you fought God. One could even say that the first time, you w-w-won. But boundless love, Tony dear, is giving you a second chance."

"Father Joe, dear Father Joe! Please! Don't do this!"

In reply he took my face in his old hands and, as he had in the first moment I ever saw him, gave me the kiss of peace.

The embrace of Father Joe led Tony Hendra on a path of restoration. His marriage was saved. Tony the satirist never became Tony the monk, but he did become Tony the father.

Stories like that of Tony Hendra remind us all to be careful with what we say about others: sometimes the exclusion we see is a tragedy surrounding the divine comedy of embracing grace.

What then is this embrace that permits us to turn from a life of self-protecting exclusion to a life of union with God and communion with others, to a life of loving God and loving others for the good of the world? The Bible calls this "faith" or "trust."

There are two parts to what the Bible means by "faith": truth-telling and embodiment. We will look at these two elements of the embrace in this and the next chapter.

TRUTH-TELLING

Humans who become restored Eikons do so first of all by identifying themselves. This is what Tony Hendra was beginning to do, what Craig Barnes's father was trying to do, and what so many are doing today. The secret to unleashing the cycle of grace in our lives is to look at God and ourselves, identify who we see, and tell the truth to God. One more time, back to Adam. You will recall that in Genesis 3 God asked Adam, "Where are you?" And Adam gave an evasive answer: "I heard the sound of you in the garden, and I was afraid, because I was naked; and I hid myself." The proper answer would have read something like this: and Adam stepped from behind the tree into the light and said, "Here I

Embracing Grace

am and this is what I did." God, it should be observed, is not interested in the facts; he's interested in an embrace of faith.

I find this matter of truth-telling to be the essence of a genuine relationship with God and with others. Fear of what might happen to the relationship can be chased away only by faith in the utter grace of God and the reciprocal love of another.

For the Christian a sense of telling the truth about oneself finds a prototype in the fifty-first Psalm, David's well-known prayer of confession. There are other examples as well: the confession at Mount Sinai at the heart of the book of Exodus, or the national confession Ezra led Israel in after the people returned from Babylon. Baptism at the hand of John in the Jordan focused on telling the truth about oneself. The biblical theme of telling God the truth about ourselves is summed up in the opening chapter of the apostle John's first letter: "If we confess our sins, he who is faithful and just will forgive us our sins and cleanse us from all unrighteousness." The simplicity of the gospel is that God promises to accept us when we give ourselves to him by telling God the truth about ourselves. The Bible calls this "confession."

Each of the great Church traditions has developed its own prayers of confession, because each knows that faith begins with truth-telling. Each of these prayers of confession is designed to be read aloud, in a community, and at the same time to probe the individual's and the community's conscience. My favorite confession, *Litany of Penitence* for Ash Wednesday, can be found in *The Book of Common Prayer* (1979). This *Litany* is one of the finest prayers of confession the Church has ever written, and can be used profitably as a routine exercise for individual introspection.

Recently, when Kris and I were saying our prayers during the Lenten season, we read *The Litany* aloud with its long inquiry into any and every sort of sin we are to confess. Kris said rather innocently about such a probing list of sins, "This is a bummer." Indeed, genuine confession explores the cracks that open up into the heart of who we are and what we have done (and not done). What we find down in those cracks is a bummer indeed, but getting down into the cracks enables us to tell the truth of our story.

That is all we need to do: tell the truth.

Before we pray the Litany together, we should observe the influence that authentic autobiographies have played in the Church. We are all aware of the sentimental biographies that have been told about so many Christian leaders, and they have their role to play. But nothing can substitute for the candid autobiographies of St. Augustine in his *Confessions,* John Bunyan's *Grace Abounding to the Chief of Sinners,* or Dorothy Day's *A Long Loneliness.* Of more recent appearance, I think of Kathleen Norris's *Dakota: A Spiritual Geography,*

James Baldwin's *Notes of a Native Son,* Lewis Smedes's *My God and I,* Randall Balmer's *Growing Pains,* or the various memoirs of Frederick Buechner. Here we find truth-tellers, and they can lead us into the cycle of grace.

But behind each of their stories is the structure of confession found in The Litany.

THE LITANY OF PENITENCE

We benefit from this prayer most if we say it aloud and if we say it slowly, letting our mind wander into the cracks of our own Eikon to discover what is there and what needs to be brought into healing grace. Telling the truth like this enables us not only to tell our own story but also to tell the inner truths of our story.

The Litany begins with the right words: we need a holy Father who will be merciful (or gracious) to us. I am asking that you pray aloud the italicized words, pausing only to reflect on the brief comments I make.

Most holy and merciful Father:

The Litany leads us next to confess both general and specific sins. It also leads us to request the mercy of God. Notice the general sins and then the specific sins, both in what we do and what we don't do. By the time we get to the end, we have found our own story.

We begin with thoughts, words, and deeds—both done and not done.

> *We confess to you and to one another,*
> *and to the whole communion of saints in heaven*
> *and on earth,*
> *that we have sinned by our own fault in thought, word,*
> *and deed;*
> *by what we have done, and by what we have left undone.*

We now move into a more comprehensive probing of low-intensity sins, such as lack of love and lack of forgiveness.

> *We have not loved you with our whole heart, and mind,*
> *and strength.*
> *We have not loved our neighbors as ourselves.*
> *We have not forgiven others, as we have been forgiven.*
> *Have mercy on us, Lord.*
> *We have been deaf to your call to serve, as Christ served us.*
> *We have not been true to the mind of Christ.*
> *We have grieved your Holy Spirit.*
> *Have mercy on us, Lord.*

Then we can think more concretely about specific sins, and we need to pause for each sin mentioned to let our minds be led to our own sins.

We confess to you, Lord, all our past unfaithfulness:
the pride, hypocrisy, and impatience of our lives,
We confess to you, Lord.
Our self-indulgent appetites and ways,
and our exploitation of other people,
We confess to you, Lord.
Our anger at our own frustration,
and our envy of those more fortunate than ourselves,
We confess to you, Lord.
Our intemperate love of worldly goods and comforts,
and our dishonesty in daily life and work,
We confess to you, Lord.
Our negligence in prayer and worship,
and our failure to commend the faith that is in us,
We confess to you, Lord.

We can now implore the Lord to accept our confession and repentance. The promise of God's embracing grace is that God accepts our prayers of confession and repentance.

Accept our repentance, Lord, for the wrongs we have done:
for our blindness to human need and suffering,
and our indifference to injustice and cruelty,
Accept our repentance, Lord.
For all false judgments, for uncharitable thoughts toward our
neighbors,

and for our prejudice and contempt
toward those who differ from us,
Accept our repentance, Lord.
For our waste and pollution of your creation,
and our lack of concern for those who come after us,
Accept our repentance, Lord.

Finally, the Litany anchors our forgiveness in God's unfailing promises and pledges holiness. One can sense the relief as our truth-telling finds God ready and willing and happy to forgive and restore and empower for a new life. This prayer can enliven the Eikon once again.

Restore us, good Lord, and let your anger depart from us;
Favorably hear us, for your mercy is great.
Accomplish in us the work of your salvation
That we may show forth your glory in the world.

By the cross and passion of your Son our Lord,
Bring us with all your saints to the joy of his resurrection.

The priest or pastor then offers this promise (and we can say it ourselves):

Almighty God, the Father of our Lord Jesus Christ,
who desires not the death of sinners,
but rather that they may turn from their wickedness and live,
has given power and commandment to his ministers to

Embracing Grace

declare and pronounce to his people, being penitent,
the absolution and remission of their sins.
He pardons and absolves all those who truly repent,
and with sincere hearts believe his holy Gospel.

Therefore we beseech him to grant us true repentance and his
Holy Spirit,
that those things may please him which we do on this day,
and that the rest of our life hereafter may be pure and holy,
so that at the last we may come to his eternal joy;
through Jesus Christ our Lord.

Amen.

I have never said this prayer without becoming conscious of sins I have committed and without looking forward to the promise of grace that comes through in the last part. Most important, I find that this prayer provokes my telling the truth of my own story and promotes a joy that God's story thereby becomes mine. I would encourage each of us to pause for a reading of this Litany aloud, listening to its words carefully so we can hear our own story in them, and then offering to God the person those words reveal us to be.

We are each like Adam and Eve, or they are like us: telling the truth is often difficult and we need help. But the Eikon can be enlivened only when we embrace ourselves in God's embrace.

LEARNING TO TELL THE TRUTH
OF OUR OWN STORY

Bob Robinson, a former pastor now working with a college ministry in northern Ohio, wrote me a letter with these words about his struggle with learning to tell his own story truthfully:

> After 40 years, I still find it extremely difficult to know the truth *about myself* and to freely admit it to myself (let alone to *God!*). I am so hard-wired with so many LIES about myself and my world and even about God that it is taking lots of time and energy and HUGE amounts of God's grace to cut through all of them. I have found that it is very difficult to really know *me!*
>
> But this [truth-telling] is the road to healing. . . . If I can understand *myself,* and then give that self to God as a sacrifice, He can take that person and do the divine work of sanctification. But until I confess (to myself *first,* as well as to God) who I am, I cannot repent from that! It is an ugly and loooooooong process.

As we try to go through this process of telling the truth about ourselves, let's remind ourselves of this: the cycle of grace comes through the simplest of means. Telling the truth about ourselves involves searching the cracks of the Eikon discovering traits in our character we thought were long forgotten, and finding cracks just recently open. But the cracks are ours, and it is the story of *our* cracks that God invites us to tell.

13
DANCING GRACE

THE EMBRACE OF FAITH, LIKE ANY EMBRACE, IS VISIBLE.

Notice how often faith in the Bible is expressed by visible verbs. Abram *moved* from Ur and set out for the Land of Promise, the children of Israel *smeared* Passover blood on the door frame, Joshua *dipped his foot* into the Jordan, David *carried* the ark to Jerusalem, the children of Israel *packed up their bags* in Babylonia and *walked all the way* to the Land of Promise. Faith isn't just something in the head and the heart;

it is something that takes hold of heart, soul, mind, and strength. It is embodied. Faith is action as much as it is assent. Faith is both embrace and embodiment.

The same visibility was found in the first century. Joseph and Mary *moved* to Egypt and then *returned* to Nazareth, John persuaded persons to get down in the Jordan *to be baptized,* Jesus *set out for Jerusalem to die,* Jesus established a memorial meal by *dispensing bread and wine* for all his followers and his followers *ingested* the bread and wine, the followers of Jesus *waited* in Jerusalem for the gift from on high, and that same Pentecostal gift *propelled them* into the Roman Empire and to the uttermost parts of the globe.

A genuine embrace is a bodily thing.

THE DANCE OF GRACE

The faith that embraces the gospel is like dancing. Since I can't dance, I know. What I see when others are dancing well I long to experience. Reared among the fundamentalists, one "advantage" I had as a teenager and adult, because we were prohibited from dancing, is that I didn't develop the knack of making a fool of myself in public by dancing ungracefully.

But the disadvantages were close behind. I will begin with the most important. Because I didn't learn to dance, I am unable to let my body become enraptured by music and sound in a graceful manner. Dancing, so I was warned as a youngster, would lead to sex. So, we were further warned, we needed to keep the body under control, and to do this we needed to stow the body under clothing, with everything all zippered and buttoned up, and one thing we were not to do was dance. Dancing, we were warned, was designed to arouse the appetites. I suppose dancing must have led to sex for people to make such a big point about it, but I wouldn't know: I didn't get to dance to find out. What I do know is that you can have one without the other. And I'll stop right there.

Dancing, good graceful dancing, is the ability of the body to express the music in such a way that actions correspond to music. For this to happen, the body needs to surrender completely to the music so that the body *becomes one with* the music. Faith, too, is the surrender of the entire person—heart, soul, mind, and strength—to the "music of the cycle of grace." To have faith or to believe—they are the same in the Bible—is to embrace God by identifying ourselves before God with utter truth, and by "fleshing it out" in real life.

The dance of grace is first of all a dance with a person: Jesus Christ.

But dancing with Jesus means dancing with the plan of God for the redemption of the world in his cross and resurrection. A holistic gospel calls for a holistic response—world, community, and the sacramental embrace of Jesus himself. In speaking

Embracing Grace

then of embracing the world, or the community of faith, or Jesus personally, we are not talking about embracing *things* but a *Person.* This is what the Bible means by receiving Christ or believing in Christ or abiding in Christ or following Christ. The work of God in the world is summed up in Jesus Christ; the community of faith is the body of Christ himself; and the sacraments are visible, physical gateways into the presence of the person of Jesus himself.

It is customary when discussing faith to begin at the personal level and move on to the community and then to the world. But in what follows I will reverse the order so we may have an opportunity to see our own personal faith as an individual instance of God's all-encompassing redemption of the created order.

FIRST EMBODIMENT: EMBRACE THE WORLD GOD IS RESTORING

The embracing dance of grace begins where God begins: with the plan to restore the whole world in Jesus Christ. Faith begins when we *embrace the world* as the sphere of God's kingdom work.

Because I have emphasized a *holistic* gospel in this book, let me observe that such a view is not the view of a few isolated cranks in the Church. The late Pope John Paul II throughout his years leading the Roman Catholic Church published encyclicals about the Christian in society, and these were then reflected upon by the bishops to compose what can only be called a brilliant treatise on the relationship of the Christian to society, *The Compendium of the Social Doctrine of the Church.* This volume shows the extension of the gospel of grace into all aspects of our world—it contains sections on human rights, social life, the family, work, economy, politics both local and global, as well as on environment and peace, as its *telos* is a "civilization of love."

In Germany, the Lutheran New Testament scholar Peter Stuhlmacher sketches a "gospel" that is nothing short of stunningly cosmic in scope, as the gospel works to liberate God's people and his creation from systemic evil so that the "one God becomes 'all in all' amid his (re)new(ed) creation."

If God's work is to redeem the entire created order, the proper response is to join in God's cosmic divine comedy. How can we embrace the world? We need to see who we are in this world and then we need to take action.

First, we begin by embracing who we are. We are Eikons which means it is our vocation to reflect the glory of God to the whole world by union with God and communion with others. In the words that many are using today, we embrace the world by being a *missional community of faith.* No one has expressed this better than Brian McLaren, the controversial but provocative and insightful author of *Generous Orthodoxy:*

"Missional faith asserts that Jesus came to preach the good news of the kingdom of God to everyone, especially the poor. He came to seek and save the lost. He came on behalf of the sick. He came to save the world. His gospel, and therefore the Christian message, is Good News for the whole world. I think the missional way is better [than the old model of separating evangelism from social action]: the gospel brings blessings to all, adherents and nonadherents alike."

If we do not begin with this "worldly" missional vision in mind we will never reach the kingdom Jesus came to establish.

Second, a restored Eikon embraces the world *locally*. I can't sit here at my computer and explain how others should embrace their world. Your world is yours, and you are invited to enter into the redemption of your world in your ways. We do this by listening, looking, learning, and linking—in our world, in our way, for our time. One pastor called me to tell me his local faith community was thinking of purchasing an old strip mall, restoring it, and using it as a holistic ministry center for the local urban community. A student told me her parents had adopted a child who had been wounded by neglect and a lack of love in an orphanage. She and her family were all praying that their hugging and touching might restore what her sister had not come to know when she most needed to know it: the love that we learn through touching.

Local needs are discovered by local eyes and local ears. Such an embodiment is as big as the world and as small as our neighborhood. We begin by focusing on the music in God's story of what God is doing in and for the world, and then we dance to the music of our faith community.

SECOND EMBODIMENT: EMBRACE OUR FAITH COMMUNITY

Some will be put off by the second form of embodiment that expresses what it means to have faith: *embrace a community of faith.* Embracing a community of faith is often called "joining a church" or "becoming a member of a church," and many today feel constricted by such requirements. But, I can't read the Bible without seeing the idea of "community" every-where, page after page. There must be thousands of verses for community to every one verse about the afterlife. Israel's community history dominates the landscape of the Bible. To extend God's promise to the world God raises up the Church of Jesus Christ, which is called the body of Christ. From the book of Acts through the end of the book of Revelation the gospel is the work of God to form a community through which God restores Eikons The apostle Paul traveled the Mediterranean founding churches, and he wrote to churches and organized churches, and Peter and John did the same. There is a lot of churchiness about the New Testament.

Perhaps you will remember how I began this book by asking what people think the gospel is, and there I mentioned three things: forgiveness of sins, justice, and the Church. We have just discussed justice (in the first embodiment) and we are now looking at the Church. Those who see the gospel in the word church are seeing a central theme of the whole Bible: God's goal for the world is the kingdom of God, and Jesus formed the Church to be a catalyst for that kingdom.

This means that one embraces oneself, God, and others by entering the community of faith. It matters that you enter into that community and make it your faith family. You can "shop" for churches today on the Internet by reading about "vision" statements and find out who is on "staff" and read about what is happening by checking out the calendar. Or, you can just start visiting churches in your area. I want to emphasize this: embracing a faith community is not an option if one is interested in the gospel that restores Eikons. Eikons are not individualists but Eikons in community.

But, embracing a faith community is more than "attending church." Church "services" are not about being "serviced by" the church. Some see church attendance as a form of entertainment—some place they go, some actions they observe, some people they watch, followed by some food at a restaurant, and then home they go. Embracing a faith community means becoming a community *participant,* and that means accepting something very important and notice-able: being the person to the community that we are meant to be. The apostle Paul calls this "spiritual gifts" in several of his letters, but whatever we want to call it we are to partic-ipate by performing what we have been gifted to do.

And it also means *ministry*—loving others because you look, listen, learn, and link up with them in their needs. Leonard Sweet, who likes to crack one-liners, says this so well: "Faith is more than beliefs to be learned; it is bonds to be lived. Faith is more than holding the 'right' beliefs; it is holding the 'right' (that is, the 'least of these') hands." A genuine community of faith is a missional community: like the many I have mentioned in this book, it sees itself as a place of grace where human beings—all kinds—can find the grace of God that can restore them to join in the kingdom of God.

It also means *trust and tolerance*—loving others for who they are, where they are in their journey, and what they might become. Too often, far too often, churches make people aware at the visceral level of "who is in" and "who is out." But, a genuine community of faith that embodies embracing grace makes it clear that the word "for" is a positive word when we say that the gospel is *for* all of us.

Now we come to personal faith, the third circle in, as embodiment.

Embracing Grace

THIRD EMBODIMENT: EMBRACE CHRIST PERSONALLY

Every time Christians gather before the Table of the Lord the individual Christian "embodies" and performs faith at a deeply personal level. We either sit or kneel; we either take a smidgeon of bread or a wafer or we are given it; the same for the cup. And we eat and drink. By eating and drinking we publicly act out our faith. The actions themselves declare our personal embrace of Jesus Christ and of the community of faith and of God's cosmic kingdom of God.

Now, as one who thinks highly of baptism, I would also maintain that the Lord's Supper and baptism are the two co-equal "first" embodiments of personal faith. Baptism, like the Lord's Supper, is a public act wherein the cracked Eikon confesses faith, acts out that faith, and experiences both the cleansing flow of embracing grace and the welcoming flow of community. Baptism, too, is a first embodiment of faith. I am aware that many baptize infants, while I am more persuaded of the adult baptism model. What I am saying about adult baptism applies, indirectly and in process, to the person who is nurtured into faith through catechism and confirmation. But the point remains the same: both the Lord's Supper and baptism are deeply personal acts of faith.

To be sure, personal faith is not limited to the Lord's Supper and baptism, which are physical acts of faith. Personal faith is an ongoing *relationship* that finds physical expression in the Church's sacraments as well as in many actions undertaken by Christians throughout the day.

WORLD, COMMUNITY, INDIVIDUAL

Again, the order of moving from world to community of faith to individual has a design. God's work is to form a community of restored Eikons for the good of others and the world. If the tendency of our culture is to focus on the individual, the tendency of the Bible is to focus on the work of God throughout the entire created order. Perhaps the order I have set out will help us see ourselves as part of God's cosmic comedy of grace.

In fact, moving from the world to the community to the individual is the Eikonic order rather than the individualistic order. If we begin with human as Eikons and see the gospel designed to restore them, then we see the gospel in holistic terms and learn that we are part of the cosmic plan of God. A short story by J. R. R. Tolkien will illustrate the point.

LEAF BY NIGGLE

Tolkien, that marvelous Roman Catholic storyteller, created

a little character named Niggle in his short story *Leaf by Niggle*. Niggle's gift in life was to make paintings on canvas of leaves. But, because he was so sensitive to the needs of the community around him, he seemed never to get his master-piece done. His painting began with a leaf, but soon the leaf was growing on a tree of some proportions, and that tree led into a forest on the edge of the mountains. Niggle was unable to finish his task because he served his neighbor, Mr. and Mrs. Parish. Not that he didn't curse them at times under his breath.

One day, well before he was done with what he thought he was called to accomplish in life, the Driver came and took him off to purgatory on the way to Eternity. In purgatory, Niggle got his act all cleaned up. Soon the Second Voice, who surely must be the Son of God, summoned Niggle deeper and higher into Eternity.

Leaf by Niggle now turns into drama. The Second Voice led Niggle into a place in Paradise where Niggle came upon the leaf in his painting as well as the other subjects of the painting: his tree and his forest and his mountain. However, in this place they were no longer a mere picture but pristine reality itself. What Niggle had dreamed of on earth, and what he was able only to approximate in his art, and what he was striving for in his own performance of the gospel, was fully realized when the Second Voice led him into the Eternal

Dream itself. When Niggle saw it all before him, now not as a picture but as living reality, he simply said, "'It's a gift!' He was referring to his art, and also to the result; but he was using the word quite literally." What he discovered was the leaves—as he imagined them, not as he had painted them. Then he realized that his gift was a participation in the big picture of God, and that he had caught a glimpse of what lay Beyond.

Niggle's gift was to dream of that Beyond with his leaf. Our performance of the gospel is to be like Niggle's, as we too are invited to live out, or embody, the gifts we have been given— even if our calling is to paint leaves, even if we are little people. If we perform the story God has given us to perform, we will hear what the Second Voice said about Niggle's not quite completed leaf: "It is the best introduction to the Mountains."

Our dance of grace, as a personal act of faith in service of the community and the world, can also be an introduction to the Mountains.

14

A FAMILY OF
EMBRACING GRACE

THE GOSPEL IS DESIGNED TO UNLEASH THE CYCLE OF GRACE
for the good of the world. When the world is filled with grace
we call it the kingdom of God. But, the kingdom of God,
because it is a vision for broken humans trying to love other
broken humans in a broken world, takes time (and more than
that).

Frederick Buechner says this perfectly: "Thus the gospel is not
only good and new but, if you take it seriously, a holy terror.
Jesus never claimed that the process of being changed from a
slob into a human being was going to be a Sunday school

picnic. On the contrary. Childbirth may occasionally be painless, but rebirth, never."

Once again, the gospel makes astounding claims: that humans can be converted from isolated and selfish individuals into God-loving Eikons whose missional focus is the good of others and the world. But, this doesn't happen overnight. It takes time, sometimes a long time, to convert individualists into Eikons.

It would be easy to finish this book with perfect examples in a perfect community of faith in a perfect world. *Pleasantville,* as it were. But, that person, that community, and that world do not (yet) exist. It is more realistic and authentic to say that most of us struggle with gospel restoration, most of us fight it, and most of us find ourselves both excluding and embracing. That means that true stories of the kingdom of God include stories of strugglers, stories of those for whom it takes time to manifest the glory of the Eikons,. One thinks here of Mike Yaconelli's *Messy Spirituality* or Lauren Winner's *Girl Meets God* or John Goldingay's *Walk On* or Parker Palmer's *Let Your Life Speak* or Anne Lamott's *Traveling Mercies* or Dr. Timothy Johnson's *Finding God in the Questions.*

Some fear that "messy" stories will glorify a messy faith. For my part, I am more afraid of a gospel that does not permit us to tell the messy story of an authentic faith.

Embracing Grace

Perhaps a biblical example will make this clear before we turn to a modern one.

THE APOSTLE JOHN

The apostle John shows that it takes a life time to become a person noted for love of others. We know of three episodes, which I discussed in *The Jesus Creed,* in John's life from the Gospels. In one he wants to shut down the ministry of an exorcist because John didn't think he was in "Jesus' denomination." In another he wants to be, along with his brother, given top billing and designated "MVP" of the Apostolic Team. And in yet another episode he asks Jesus to do to the Samaritan villages, who have not responded all-at-once with a falling-heads-over-heels kind of love for his kingdom preaching, what God had done once-upon-a-time but long-ago to Sodom and Gomorrah. Here are three separate incidents about John, and in each one of them he is anything but loving toward others, and he seems not at all to care for the world.

But, by the time John settles into dipping his quill into ink to write his first letter, his quill somehow is stuck on the word "love," and he spends an entire letter trying to figure out new ways to talk about love. The difference between those three early episodes in his life and the letter he wrote much later is dramatic. It is the story of a growing love, of the conversion of a total person to a holistic gospel.

Here is my point: John didn't suddenly wake up one day early in his journey with Jesus and decide to become a loving man and then presto! it just happened. It took him a lifetime to learn to be loving. No one who came into contact with John would have experienced the kingdom for some time (just ask the Samaritans!).

Let's just guess that John was a young man when he tried to get Samaria to turn back the wheels of history three-quarters of a millennium and turn back to the traditional faith of Israel, and let's also guess that he was an old man when he wrote his first letter. And, let's just guess that the John of that love letter didn't arrive on the scene immediately after the Resurrection and Pentecost, though he may have. It took John some time, at least the three years he was with Jesus and almost certainly many more, to become a loving man. It takes time to restore an Eikon because the cracks are big and deep and it takes a while for humans to rummage around in them to learn what is there. To learn to tell the truth of our own cracks takes time.

But restoration, however long, is what the story of embracing grace is all about. If you've ever restored an antique or a wall or a machine, you know that the process is often messy. The same is often true with humans who are set on their journey toward God and others in this messy world of ours. But it happens.

When one person is transformed we see the kingdom of God; and when we see an entire family and a whole community transformed we see even more of the kingdom.

KINGDOM: THE JESUS VERSION

What does it look like, this kingdom that Jesus preached and looked for? I find this question to be at the very center of what the gospel is all about. How did Jesus envision that kingdom? What did he say about it? What was the shape of the life he tried to create for those closest to him? Those are central gospel questions.

I begin with the stirring conclusion of Miroslav Volf, whose statement here sums up the entire message of the Bible about kingdom as expressed in three terms: love, peace, and justice. Volf contends that, in this fallen and broken world, all justice is tied into injustices. So . . .

> If you want justice and nothing but justice, you will inevitably get injustice. If you want justice without injustice, you must want love. A world of perfect justice is a world of love. It is a world with no "rules," in which everyone does what he or she pleases and all are pleased by what everyone does; a world of no "rights" because there are no wrongs from which to be protected; a world of no "legitimate entitlements," because everything is given and nothing withheld; a world with no "equality" because all differences

are loved in their own appropriate way; a world in which "desert" plays no role because all actions stem from super-abundant grace. . . . The blindfold would be taken from the eyes of *Justitia* and she would delight in whatever she saw; she would lay aside the scales because she would not need to weigh and compare anything; she would drop her sword because there would be nothing to police.

Volf has the biblical message in his grasp: the kingdom of God is about one's relationship with God and with others and with creation.

This kingdom of Jesus involves a revolutionary reordering of society. As Volf suggests, genuine equality is not the elimination of difference. In fact, God delights in difference—check out creation itself: we've got elephants and humming-birds, mountains that stretch into the heavens and valleys that plummet into the deeps of the earth, we've got rivers always going somewhere and we've got deserts that have been there forever, we've got women and we've got men (and adolescents who are somewhere in between), and we've got humans of all kinds of colors and shapes and sizes. In God's equality, difference is maintained and loved. So, Jesus invited all sorts to his table—tax collectors and sinners and women and lepers and thieves and adulterers and adulteresses and good old-fashioned upright people sitting with those whose lives had tarnished their God-given glory. Jesus' kingdom is a

Embracing Grace

radical reorientation of society because it does not care about difference. It cares about the mission to restore.

And so, when Jesus gave his first sermon at his hometown synagogue, as we now read it in the fourth chapter of the Gospel of Luke, this is what he said the kingdom would bring:

> The Spirit of the Lord is upon me,
> > because he has anointed me
> > > to bring good news to the poor.
> He has sent me to proclaim release to the captives
> > and recovery of sight to the blind,
> > > to let the oppressed go free,
> to proclaim the year of the Lord's favor.

Evidently, as shown in this inaugural sermon when Jesus set out his favorite themes, the kingdom would look like this: all will be included; poverty will end; oppressive powers will be leveled; the imprisoned will discover a door that leads to freedom; the physically challenged will wake up with new gifts; and the Lord's favor will skip and dance through the land. This is Jesus' gospel of the kingdom. Anything less than this is less than Jesus' gospel.

But, we gain only glimpses of the kingdom in this life.

Why? Because Eikon restoration takes time, sometimes a life time. Sometimes the pain is so deep and the wounds so damaging that it takes a lifetime for a cracked Eikon to be burnished and gleaming so that it can blaze forth with God's brilliant glory. But God's embracing grace can make Eikons brilliant.

GOD'S RESTORING, EMBRACING GRACE

God's story of embracing grace is not always that of immediate miracles and sudden transformations. More often, it is the gradual healing of a cracked Eikon so that a person finds herself or himself in a story one day where the person is healthy, is helping others, and is working to heal a hurting world. Some people suggest that we can be restored in a blink, but (frankly) it doesn't happen like that very often. For most people it is like the experience of Karen Spears Zacharias, who tells her story in the book *Hero Mama* that has been re-issued in paperback as *After the Flag is Folded*. I want to close *Embracing Grace* by looking at the life of one person who is in the process of restoration along with her family and her community—in fact, the world of which she is a part. She illustrates a holistic gospel that can take hold of a person and work its way outward—over time.

In July of 1966 a Jeep pulled up to the Spears's trailer in Rogersville, Tennessee, and ruined a family. David Spears, a soldier in Vietnam, was the father; Shelby was the mother;

the three kids were Frank, Karen, and Linda. A soldier got out of the Jeep and informed Shelby that Dave had been killed in the central highlands of Vietnam. As Karen puts it in her memoir, "Before his death, ours was a home filled with intimacy and devotion. After his death, it was filled with chaos and destruction."

It was chaos, as in the tohu va-bohu. Shelby sought for love in the bodies of men and suppressed her anger and fears with alcohol and drugs. Frank's anger turned into violence, and he was sent away to a military school, found drugs, enrolled in the armed forces, ended up in Fort Leavenworth's prison, and then discovered the good news of God's love. Linda suffered the least. Karen struggled with a sassy temperament and self-determination. When Charlie (her youth pastor) and his wife left for another church, Karen's world was rocked. She compensated for this loss by searching for love in the wrong place—in the arms of a young kid who was not her equal, in a relationship she knew was not right, and in a lifestyle that could not satisfy. Amidst all this chaos, Karen discovered the grace of God, but it took time for her to recover from a mess at home, a pregnancy, an abortion, and plenty of soul-misery.

But restoration can happen, and *Hero Mama* is a testament of one woman's journey and a family's restoration, and of how her own restoration has enabled Karen to speak on a national platform about how the children of killed military persons can recover. The restoration began with her relationship with her brother. Years after the abortion her brother opposed, Karen sought out Frank to apologize.

"I need to ask your forgiveness for something," I said (to Frank).

Frank leaned up against the door to my Toyota and crossed his arms over his barrel chest. "I'm listening," he said.

"I'm sorry I had that abortion," I said. "I wish I'd listened to you. But I was angry with you. I didn't think you had any right to tell me what to do with my life. I was wrong. You were right."

"I made mistakes, too, Karen," Frank said. "I messed a lot of things up. I understand why you were angry with me. I don't blame you for being mad."

Then he reached over and wrapped me up in a big bear hug. Forgiveness is something our family has learned to embrace. We've had to.

This newly discovered cycle of grace included her mother:

. . . for all Mama's faults, for all of mine, I realized that the best decision Daddy ever made was asking Shelby Jean Mayes to marry him and to have his babies.

Karen has become a national spokesperson for Vietnam survivors and veterans. She has spoken at the Vietnam

Veteran's Memorial in Washington, D.C., and she is soon to speak at the national Veteran's Day celebration. All because she learned that the embrace of grace can heal wounds and give the courage to extend grace to others.

Perhaps what I like most about Karen's story is its lucid honesty of the struggles she has known—no one holds her up as a model of perfection. What we do see is what this book is all about: the gospel is the work of God to restore Eikons in the context of a community for the good of others and the world. That work of God may be powerful but it takes time.

GRACE ONE MORE TIME

Grace, as Frederick Buechner defines it, is like God saying this to each one of us: "'Here is your life. You might never have been, but you *are,* because the party wouldn't have been complete without you. Here is the world. Beautiful and terrible things will happen. Don't be afraid. I am with you. Nothing can ever separate us. It's for you I created the universe. I love you.'

"There's only one catch," Buechner continues. "Like any other gift, the gift of grace can be yours only if you'll reach out and take it.

"Maybe being able to reach out and take it is a gift too."

Niggle knew it was a gift; Karen knows it is a gift; Jesus offers it to us as a gift.

"Take," Jesus says, "embrace me."

O God,

you have taught us to keep all your commandments by loving
you and our neighbors:
Grant us the grace of your Holy Spirit, that we may be
devoted to you with our whole heart,
and united to others with pure affection;
through Jesus Christ our Lord,
who lives and reigns with you and the Holy Spirit,
one God,
for ever and ever.
Amen.

Book of Common Prayer
Collect for the Season after Pentecost
Proper 9

ACKNOWLEDGMENTS

I am grateful to friends and colleagues who have read parts or all of *Embracing Grace*: Keith Carpenter, Paul Duppenthaler, John Ortberg, Brad Nassif, Bob Robinson, Garry Poole, Doug Halsne, Mark Albrecht, Ken White, Greg Clark, Hans Boersma, Steve McCoy, Joe Modica, Vince Bacote, and Don Richmond. I remain grateful to North Park University and to its board for creating an environment of embracing grace. I record my gratitude here especially to the kindnesses of Dean Charles Peterson. Also I am grateful to a student Renee Dinges who read and commented extensively on *Embracing Grace*.

To Miroslav Volf I offer my deepest appreciation for writing what is the most profound theological book I've read in years: *Exclusion and Embrace.*

I dedicate this book, in a big family embrace, to our two children and their wonderful mates. As always, my wife, Kris, is part of everything I write and do, and perhaps more in a book about embracing grace than anything I've written.

Not enough can be said about my editor, Lil Copan. She is a literary artist, and I consider myself fortunate to be graced by her embracing eye and green pen. And she reads baseball books! And the good folk at Paraclete, too many to name—but I will mention Lillian Miao, Carol Showalter, Jenny Lynch, Gail Gibson, Sister Mercy, Laura McKendree, Ron Minor, Bob Edmonson, and countless others there who see publishing as the leaf they are to paint.

WORKS CITED

Works cited are listed below with pages from which I quote. If a full title is given in the text, it is not listed here.

Augustine. *The Confessions* (trans. P. Burton; New York: A. A. Knopf, 2001), 5 (from 1.1.1).

Auxentios: I found this quotation in D. Fairbairn, *Eastern Orthodoxy through Western Eyes* (Louisville, Ky: Westminster John Knox, 2002), 74.

Barnes, C. *Searching for Home: Spirituality for Restless Souls* (Grand Rapids, Mich.: Brazos, 2003), 9–13, 17.

Bell, Rob. *Velvet Elvis: Repainting the Christian Faith* (Grand Rapids: Zondervan, 2005), 147.

Berry, W. *Sex, Economy, Freedom, and Community* (New York: Pantheon, 1993), 20.

Buechner, F. *Beyond Words* (San Francisco: HarperSanFrancisco, 2004), 137.
The Sacred Journey and *Now and Then* and *Telling Secrets* and *The Eyes of the Heart* (San Francisco: HarperSanFrancisco, 1982, 1983, 1991, 1999).

Burke, J. *No Perfect People Allowed: Creating a Come As You Are Culture in the Church* (Grand Rapids: Zondervan, 2005).

Carlson, P. See Lois Carlson Bridges, *Monganga Paul: The Congo Ministry and Martyrdom of Paul Carlson, M.D.* (2d ed.; Chicago: Covenant Publications, 2004); quotations from pp. 137-138, 152-153.

Chesterton, G. K. *On Lying in Bed, and Other Essays* (Calgary: Bayeux Arts, 2000), 457 ("The Priest of Spring").

Cruden, Alexander. See Julia Keay, *Alexander the Corrector: The Tormented Genius who Unwrote the Bible* (New York: HarperCollins, 2004).

Delbanco, A. *The Real American Dream: A Meditation on Hope* (Cambridge, Mass: Harvard University Press, 1999), 105.

DeYoung, C., with M. O. Emerson, G. Yancey, K. Chai Kim, *United by Faith: The Multiracial Congregation as an Answer to the Problem of Race* (New York: Oxford University Press, 2003).

Doyle, B. *The Wet Engine* (Brewster, Mass: Paraclete, 2005), 132.

Durrwell, F. X. *Christ Our Passover: The Indispensable Role of Resurrection in Our Salvation* (trans. J. F. Craghan; Liguori, Mo.: Liguori, 2004), 56.

Elie, P. *The Life You Save May Be Your Own: An American Pilgrimage* (New York: Farrar, Straus, and Giroux, 2003).

Etzioni, A. "Individualism—Within History," *The Hedgehog Review* 4 (2002): 49–56, here p. 49.

Edwards, J. *Charity and Its Fruits* (Works of Jonathan Edwards, volume 8: *Ethical Writings*; ed. P. Ramsey; New Haven: Yale University Press, 1989), pp. 123–397.

Freeman, P. *St. Patrick of Ireland: A Biography* (New York: Simon & Schuster, 2004).

Hendra, T. *Father Joe: The Man Who Saved My Soul* (New York: Random 2004), 177-178, 244-245. I am grateful to my friend Father Rob Merola for pointing me to this book.

Hollingsworth, A. *The Simple Faith of Mister Rogers: Spiritual Insights from the World's Most Beloved Neighbor* (Nashville: Integrity, 2005), xxiii, 83, 9, xxvi.

Lewis, C. S. *The Weight of Glory and Other Addresses* (Grand Rapids: Eerdmans, 1973), 14-15.

Marsden, G. *Jonathan Edwards: A Life* (New Haven: Yale University Press, 2003), 191, 443.

McCarthy, M. *Memories of a Catholic Girlhood* (New York: Harcourt, Brace, 1957), 19, 27. See F. Kiernan, *Seeing Mary Plain: A Life of Mary McCarthy* (New York: W. W. Norton, 2000), 51-52, 704–742.

McLaren, B. *Generous Orthodoxy* (Grand Rapids: Zondervan, 2004), 110-111, 232.

McLaren, B. *The Story We Find Ourselves In: Further Adventures of a New Kind of Christian* (San Francisco: Jossey-Bass, 2003).

Mencken, H. L. *A Mencken Chrestomathy* (New York: A. A. Knopf, 1976), 5-6.

Pagitt, D. *Reimagining Spiritual Formation* (Grand Rapids: Zondervan, 2004), 25, 96-97.

Piper, J. *Desiring God* (Sisters, Oregon: Multnomah, 2003).

Plantinga, C. *Not the Way It's Supposed to Be: A Breviary of Sin* (Grand Rapids: Eerdmans, 1995), 5, 14, 16.

Robinson, M. *Gilead* (New York: Farrar, Straus, Giroux, 2004), 9, 57.

Shirer, W.L. *Love and Hatred: The Troubled Marriage of Leo and Sonya Tolstoy* (New York: Simon and Schuster, 1994), 13, 259.

Sider, R., with P. N. Olson, H. R. Unruh, *Churches that Make a Difference: Reaching Your Community with Good News and Good Works* (Grand Rapids: Baker Books, 2002), which is based on R. J. Sider, *Good News and Good Works: A Theology of the Whole Gospel* (Grand Rapids: Baker Books, 1993).

Speckhard, P. A. "Who Made Thee?" *Touchstone* (January/February, 2005), 13-14.

Stuhlmacher, P. *Revisiting Paul's Doctrine of Justification* (Downers Grove, Ill.: IVP, 2001), 53.

Sweet, L. *Out of the Question—Into the Mystery: Getting Lost in the GodLife Relationship* (Colorado Springs: Waterbrook, 2004), 21.

Tarkington, B. *Penrod and Sam* (Bloomington, Ind.: Indiana University Press, 2003), 107.

Tolkien, J. R. R. *Tree and Leaf* (Boston: Houghton Mifflin, 1989), 75–95.

Tolstoy, L. *A Confession*, in *The Portable Tolstoy* (ed. J. Bayley; New York: Penguin, 1978), 666–731.

Tubman, H. See Catherine Clinton, *Harriet Tubman: The Road to Freedom* (New York: Little, Brown, 2004), pp. 19, 13, 32, 203.

Vanhoozer, K. "The Atonement in Postmodernity: Guilt, Goats, and Gifts," in *The Glory of the Atonement: Biblical, Historical, and Practical Perspectives* (Downers Grove, Ill.: IVP, 2004), 367–404, quoting from 378, 404.

Volf, M. *Exclusion and Embrace: A Theological Exploration of Identity, Otherness, and Reconciliation* (Nashville, Tennessee: Abingdon, 1996), 87, 223.

Webber, R. *The Younger Evangelicals: Facing the Challenges of the New World* (Grand Rapids: Baker Books, 2002), 113. I am grateful to Bob Robinson for pointing me to this quotation.

Wesley, J. *John Wesley* (ed. A. C. Outler; New York: Oxford University Press, 1980), 195.

Yancey, Philip. *What's So Amazing about Grace?* (Grand Rapids: Zondervan, 1997).

Zacharias, Karen Spears. *Hero Mama: A Daughter Remembers the Father She Lost in Vietnam—and the Mother Who Held Her Family Together* (New York: William Morrow, 2005), 14, 263-264, 360.

ABOUT PARACLETE PRESS

WHO WE ARE

Paraclete Press is an ecumenical publisher of books on Christian spirituality for people of all denominations and backgrounds.

We publish books that represent the wide spectrum of Christian belief and practice—Catholic, Orthodox, and Protestant.

We market our books primarily through booksellers; we are what is called a "trade" publisher, which means that we like it best when readers buy our books from booksellers, our partners in successfully reaching as wide an audience as possible.

We are uniquely positioned in the marketplace without connection to a large corporation or conglomerate and with informal relationships to many branches and denominations of faith, rather than a formal relationship to any single one. We focus on publishing a diversity of thoughts and perspectives—the fruit of our diversity as a company.

WHAT WE ARE DOING

Paraclete Press is publishing books that show the diversity and depth of what it means to be Christian. We publish books that reflect the Christian experience across many cultures, time periods, and houses of worship.

We publish books about spiritual practice, history, ideas, customs, and rituals, and books that nourish the vibrant life of the church.

We have several different series of books within Paraclete Press, including the bestselling Living Library series of modernized classic texts, A Voice from the Monastery—giving voice to men and women monastics on what it means to live a spiritual life today, and Many Mansions—for exploring the riches of the world's religious traditions and discovering how other faiths inform Christian thought and practice.

Learn more about us at our website:
www.paracletepress.com, or call us toll-free at
1-800-451-5006.

ALSO AVAILABLE FROM PARACLETE PRESS

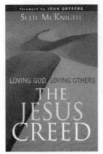

The Jesus Creed
Scot McKnight
ISBN: 1-55725-400-1
335 pages
$16.95, Trade Paper

In this practical, story-filled, witty, and illuminating volume, Scot McKnight gives Christians an opportunity to walk alongside Jesus as he teaches the Jesus Creed–the amended Jewish Shema–of love of the Father and love of others.

"For a long time [Scot McKnight] has been a kind of secret weapon for my own education and growth. Now he can be yours as well. This book will bring Jesus' world and yours much closer together."
—John Ortberg, author of
If You Want to Walk on Water, You've Got to Get Out of the Boat

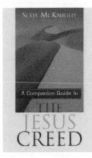

A Companion Guide to The Jesus Creed
Scot McKnight
ISBN: 1-55725-412-5
67 pages
$5.95

Designed for group or individual use, this companion guide is perfect for Bible study groups, classes, or personal devotions. Each of the thirty sessions begins with reciting the *Jesus Creed* and ends with the Lord's Prayer. In between, Scot McKnight helps you follow the *Jesus Creed* in your life through reflections that summarize the theme of each chapter, prayers, exercises, and Scriptures that invite you to delve more deeply into the *Jesus Creed*.

Available from most booksellers or through Paraclete Press
www.paracletepress.com
1-800-451-5006
Try your local bookstore first.